Nancy Leigh DeMoss and Tim Grissom have produced a magnificent interactive study for those who want to go deeper with God, and experience Christ's grace and empowerment in every area of their lives. *Seeking Him* will help you examine yourself in light of Scripture. It will take you to God's throne, where you'll realize He alone can meet your deepest needs, and He alone is worthy of your worship. I highly recommend this work.

RANDY ALCORN
Eternal Perspective Ministries

There is nothing sweeter than having been cleansed by God's Spirit through the Word of God. It truly does bring freedom from all else except pleasing Him. If you don't know how to find this in the Word of God, then *Seeking Him* is the study you need. Nancy and Tim will take you by the hand and lead you into the presence of our Holy God where you'll long to be holy even as He is holy.

KAY ARTHUR
Precept Ministries International

The work from Nancy Leigh DeMoss and Tim Grissom, *Seeking Him*, will be treasured by many. DeMoss and Grissom lay out a path to intimacy clearly, examine wonderful Scriptures, tell encouraging stories, exegete the human condition forthrightly, and generally help to make the hard work a sweet endeavor.

ROBERT O. BAKKE
National Day of Prayer

Life Action has been used of God for many years to bring timely messages in countless churches on all aspects of the biblical essentials for true revival. Here is the essence of their message, that God has used so mightily. That we may see a full revival in our day that may well save our nation, this book is crucial—especially for pastors and other leaders of God's people. No words are adequate to encourage every Christian to process their relationship with God with the timely help of this book.

HENRY BLACKABY
Blackaby Ministries International

The church has a great task before it—to let the world know the true God. Nonbelievers desperately need to see in us the reality of His holiness, grace, and saving power. *Seeking Him* is an excellent resource to help the church fulfill that calling. This study is revealing and penetrating; it leads believers to identify areas of personal inconsistency in their walk with God, and can't help but inspire a desire for greater holiness and commitment to our Savior.

VONETTE BRIGHT
Campus Crusade for Christ

America's organized prayer movements have multiplied in the last few years; yet, amazingly, the church today is being run increasingly like a business, and the lifestyle of its members is often subconsciously becoming more and more like the world. In both the Old and New Testaments when God's people strayed, He always called them back to Himself and His holiness through repentance and revival.

You are holding in your hands a book that contains the first step God has used for centuries to confront His own children with their unrecognized sins—calling them to personal and collective repentance and renewal. Historically this always has been the starting point of all culture-changing revivals.

The revival fires He longs to fan into your city, nation, and the world will have been ignited—to be spread by the Holy Spirit—until we once again experience a sweeping revival like the 1904–05 Welsh Revival.

EVELYN CHRISTENSON
Author, Speaker

Nancy Leigh DeMoss and Tim Grissom have produced a timely and very accessible interactive study guide for revival. This can be invaluable to both individuals and churches. How desperately we need God's renewing power to work through us. I can highly recommend this.

CHARLES W. COLSON
Prison Fellowship

Nancy Leigh DeMoss writes with great conviction about the real answer to the spiritual problems confronting us. If you are tired of religious fads and Band-Aid solutions, let *Seeking Him* draw you near to the God who abundantly supplies grace on every level of our lives.

JIM CYMBALA
The Brooklyn Tabernacle

When Nancy spoke to our staff years ago, her message sparked a revival unlike any our movement has ever experienced. She continues to be one of today's leading teachers on personal and corporate revival.

STEVE DOUGLASS
Campus Crusade for Christ

The new revival resource, *Seeking Him* is a positive effort to providing a tool for this to take place. You and your church will be immeasurably blessed. God will be honored, and revival will be nearer as you prayerfully study this significant resource. May God bless you in your personal search for revival.

JAMES T. DRAPER JR.
Former president of the Southern Baptist Convention and LifeWay Christian Resources

Seeking Him is quite simply the most practical, concise guide to personal and corporate revival that I've ever seen. Nancy Leigh DeMoss and Tim Grissom have developed a Holy Spirit–anointed tool that quickens the life of God in our hearts and makes revival a reality that can happen now. Get ready for revival!

DICK EASTMAN
Every Home for Christ

Everybody is talking about revival, but seldom have we seen a clear step-by-step guide to experiencing personal and corporate revival. This is every pastor's dream. Finally! A guide to assist every member in personal revival and every church in corporate revival.

TONY EVANS
Oak Cliff Bible Fellowship

More than anything else in life, seeking the presence of God ought to be foremost. In this guide Nancy and Tim will help you overcome your personal obstacles to seeking Him and set you on a path for a fresh and unique experience with God.

LOIS I. EVANS
Pastors' Wives Network

Life Action Ministries has stayed true to their calling by praying faithfully, laboring earnestly, and diligently providing resources in the hope that God would awaken the church to renewed, vibrant life in Christ. Their ministry has impacted me personally. *Seeking Him* helps identify the obstacles to genuine revival and lovingly leads the reader out of the fog of deception, the lethargy of lost intimacy, and the chains of addictions, into the joy God intends for His people.

STEVE GREEN
Christian Recording Artist

This is a welcome tool for all who yearn for a fresh movement of God in our day. It dares us to take up the psalmist's challenge to seek God and let our own hearts revive—and then to pray for a spiritual awakening of such magnitude that our homes, communities, cities, and nations are indelibly changed. Oh that God may rend the heavens, reveal His glory, and renew and revive His Sleeping Beauty, the Church! This study rings out a call to help rouse her from her sleep.

MARY KASSIAN
Author, Speaker, Theologian

An excellent mix of Scripture, stories of personal renewal, and counsel on how to deal with sin in one's life. To confront the truth found here is to face the loving, chastening, and transforming person of God's Holy Spirit. I pray that multitudes will take the risk and expose themselves.

DENNIS F. KINLAW
The Francis Asbury Society

Seeking Him is a grace gift from God to me and to His people. Don't think of it as just another book. Use the questions to help you and your friends face God . . . heart to heart. Ask Him to speak to you in the depths of your life, and trust Him to answer your prayer. This book will revive your faith and inner life with God. It will inspire your heart to sing and your feet to dance. I will be surprised if you do not weep inwardly and genuinely, pray with new passion, and even shout with joy. And you will want everyone you know to meet God in fresh and life-changing ways through reading it. God is already using *Seeking Him* as a gentle but mighty and decisive weapon to bring revival "for such a time as this."

JERRY KIRK
National Coalition for the Protection of Children & Families

There are great two misconnects to enjoying personal revival—the misconnect of our heads with God and the misconnect of our hearts with Him.

In *Seeking Him*, Nancy Leigh DeMoss and Tim Grissom gently but convincingly demonstrate that personal revival comes when our head and heart meet God with holy conviction through His Word. Whether you're new in the faith or have been around awhile, this connection and the personal revival that results is worth pursing vigorously. *Seeking Him* is a loving, instructive road map to that goal.

WOODROW KROLL
Back to the Bible

Seeking Him is a refreshing, biblically based practical resource that engages the heart, the mind, and the will to pursue the "lover of our souls". . . It is a wonderfully written, balanced study that challenges the heart without being emotionally manipulative.

CRAWFORD W. LORITTS JR.
Fellowship Bible Church

Here is a helpful plan of study to accelerate your spiritual growth. It is thoroughly biblical, easy to use, and targeted for all those of us who want to apply the principles of revival to our individual lives. Here are the keys to a closer walk with God that are accessible for those whose hearts hunger for deeper fellowship with the Savior.

ERWIN W. LUTZER
The Moody Church

How do you know when you are experiencing revival? When your focus is on God and not yourself. Nancy Leigh DeMoss' work *Seeking Him* gets it right. Step-by-step, she directs willing hearts in how to turn from self and how to seek Him. And what will you find? God seeking you—relentlessly pursuing you, pleading with you to find His promised joy and satisfaction in Him alone.

JAMES MACDONALD
Harvest Bible Chapel

There is no question that the Christian community desperately needs the spiritual revival that *Seeking Him* offers. I pray that the revival they are working for comes soon.

DENNIS RAINEY
FamilyLife

Revival is nothing less than God manifesting Himself in the midst of His people. When God shows Himself to His people they experience holiness in their hearts, passionate love in their spirits, and spiritual fire in their bones that exceed any precious spiritual experiences previously known. This is the greatest need of today's church! Millions of individuals and tens of thousands of churches need to make seeking God's face their primary endeavor and to persist in this labor of love until God comes and rains righteousness upon us. This manual will help. Use it I plead, for God's glory and the world's good.

RICHARD OWEN ROBERTS
International Awakening Ministries

Many talk about revival but few help Christians to understand and know how to experience revival personally. However, Nancy Leigh DeMoss has done it. She has constructed an interactive, biblically sound way for a person to work through the issues of revival. I especially like the small group format, which enables a person to apply the material to their lives but also to do it in the larger context of community. Any church or individual that is serious about revival should purchase this book.

DALE SCHLAFER
Center for World Revival & Awakening

Seeking Him is a welcome release for all of us who continue to trust that God will answer our prayers for revival. It will reward you with a deeper walk with Christ and position your life to be used greatly by Him.

JOSEPH M. STOWELL
Cornerstone University

A nationwide revival is extremely personal. In fact, so personal it begins with you and me. *Seeking Him* provides an intimate and insightful guide to holy living, a heaven-blessed soul, and a happy heart that can't help but be on fire for the Lord Jesus!

JONI EARECKSON TADA
Joni and Friends

Seeking**Him**

Experiencing the **Joy** of Personal Revival

A 12-Week Study for Individual and Group Use

"You who seek God, let your hearts revive."
PSALM 69:32b

Nancy Leigh DeMoss
and Tim Grissom
with Life Action Ministries

MOODY PUBLISHERS
CHICAGO

All italics for emphasis in Scripture verses have been added by author.

Interior design: Smartt Guys design
Cover Design: LeVan Fisher Design
Cover Photo: Ilker Ender, photographer

ISBN: 978-0-8024-1362-8

We hope you enjoy this book from Moody Publishers. Our goal is to provide high-quality, thought-provoking books and products that connect truth to your real needs and challenges. For more information on other books and products written and produced from a biblical perspective, go to www.moodypublishers.com or write to:

Moody Publishers
820 N. LaSalle Boulevard
Chicago, IL 60610

3 5 7 9 10 8 6 4 2

Printed in the United States of America

CONTENTS

ACKNOWLEDGMENTS

Seeking Him is the result of a collaborative effort that has gone through multiple stages over more than a decade. The final product is the fruit of the investment of many individuals, particularly the following:

- *Del Fehsenfeld Jr.*—from 1971 when he founded Life Action Ministries until his homegoing as a result of a brain tumor in 1989, Del modeled, preached, and taught the principles that form the basis for *Seeking Him.*
- *Life Action Ministries revivalists and staff* developed and shaped many of the concepts presented in this material.
- *Claude King* contributed valuable ideas and input to the early "birthing" stages.
- *Eric Stanford* edited an early version and wrote some of the sidebar material.
- *The Moody Publishers team* "resurrected" a project that had been shelved for several years and provided the impetus to bring it to publication.
- *Dawn Wilson* provided substantial research.
- *Mary Horner Collins* reformatted the material and provided significant editorial input.
- *Mike Neises* served as the production coordinator for the most recent writing/editing stage.
- *Tim Grissom* has been involved with the development of this study from the outset. He wrote the Faith-Builder Stories, based on interviews with the individuals whose testimonies are shared; he also wrote substantial portions of the Truth Encounter material.
- *Nancy Leigh DeMoss* wrote most of the Making It Personal sections and substantial portions of the Truth Encounter material; she served as the senior writer and editor for the final version.

Since 1971 teams from Life Action Ministries have conducted more than 1,200 extended revival meetings in local churches. With one exception, the "Faith-Builder Stories" throughout this book are true accounts of individuals who experienced personal revival in the context of those meetings. (The Faith-Builder story in lesson 12 is by coauthor Tim Grissom.) All names in the Faith-Builder stories have been changed, except for Tim and his late wife, Janiece.

For more information about Life Action Ministries or to inquire about scheduling a team in your church, contact Life Action Ministries, P.O. Box 31, Buchanan, MI, 49107; 269/684-5905; e-mail: info@lifeaction.org; www.lifeaction.org.

INTRODUCTION

Are you tired of trying to be a good Christian? Are you overloaded and worn out with church activities? Do you sometimes feel as if you're just going through the motions of the Christian life? Do you often find yourself running on empty spiritually? Do you experience heaviness or shame more than joy and freedom in your Christian life? If you answered yes to any of these questions, then perhaps God is calling you to something deeper. Maybe you're ready to experience personal revival!

Welcome to *Seeking Him,* an interactive study designed to lead you into a revived relationship with our loving heavenly Father. God wants to reveal Himself to you; He wants to fill your heart with Himself; He wants to set you free from every unholy passion; He wants you to drink deeply of the joys found in His presence; He wants your service for Him to be the overflow of genuine love and an authentic life; He wants you to be a reflector of His glory in our dark world. He wants you—and His entire church—to be revived!

Clarifying Terms

Depending on your background, the word *revival* may carry some baggage or sound like an old-fashioned concept. *Revival* is a label that has been applied to a variety of happenings, including an annual series of religious meetings, evangelistic campaigns, seasons of increased religious fervor, and moral and social reformation.

While all these elements may be present in times of revival, they don't adequately get to the heart of true revival. Revival is not an *event* we can schedule on the calendar. Nor is it synonymous with *evangelism,* though when revival comes, unbelievers will be converted and born into God's family. Further, though our emotions will be involved, revival should not be confused with mere *emotionalism*. And though there is nothing more exciting than the church's being alive with God's presence, revival cannot necessarily be equated with the intense *excitement* and *enthusiasm* we see being experienced in many large Christian gatherings today.

So what is revival, really? Who is it for? Do we have any influence over when and where it takes place? How can we know if it's genuine? You will explore these and other questions as you work through this study.

The word *revive* literally means "to bring back to life." For our purposes in this book we will use a simple definition: Revival is what happens when God's people, whether individually or corporately, are restored to a right relationship with Him. Revival is a supernatural work of God—it is not something we can manufacture or package. In times of personal or corporate revival, God's people experience His presence and power in ways previously missing from their lives and to degrees never thought possible. A revived church is the greatest means of making God's great redemptive plan known throughout our world.

In his book *Revival,* Richard Owen Roberts observes:

> Despite the tremendous amount of activity found in religious circles today, there is a very real sense in which the Church itself is like a sleeping giant.... When revival comes, the giant will not only stir and awaken, but also move with dynamic power and glorious impact. Can you imagine the entire Body of Christ moving throughout the earth with unified purpose and Holy Spirit power?....Unleash all this transforming power against the forces of sin and evil in your community. That is what revival is.[1]

In times of revival, God's people experience His presence and power to degrees never thought possible. A revived church is the greatest means of making God's great redemptive plan known throughout our world.

Roberts's description of revival as the awakening of a sleeping giant—the church—has been borne out in some remarkable seasons in history—moments when God sovereignly revealed His glory and released the power of His Spirit in an unusual way, in and through His church. The release of *Seeking Him* was timed to commemorate the 100th anniversary of one such divine visitation.

Glimpses of His Glory

The turn of the twentieth century was marked by an unusual concern for spiritual matters. Believers throughout the world were moved to pray for revival. In November 1904, the Spirit of God began to stir in an extraordinary way in the hearts of believers throughout the Principality of Wales. What transpired over the next several months was nothing short of supernatural.

"Bend the Church, and save the world!" was the cry that rang out through villages and towns, in the churches, and in the hearts of men, women, children, and young people throughout all of Wales.

"Bend the Church, and save the world!" ***was the cry that rang out through villages and towns . . . throughout all of Wales.***

Evan Roberts was one human instrument that God used in this season of revival. The fire of God burned in the heart of this twenty-six-year-old coal miner who had little formal education. Everywhere he went, Evan Roberts delivered a message that was simple, straightforward, and timeless. It became known as "The Four Points." Did God's people desire an outpouring of His Spirit? Then four conditions must be observed:

- Confess all known sin.
- Put away all doubtful things and forgive everyone.
- Obey the promptings of the Holy Spirit.
- Publicly confess Christ as your Savior.

One of the marked characteristics of the Welsh Revival was an inescapable sense of the presence of God. Church services that had been cold and formal began to throb with new life. Believers and unbelievers alike came under intense conviction of sin; confession and restitution—sometimes costly—became the order of the day. Churches were crowded day and night—not in response to promotion or advertising efforts or celebrity speakers—but as people were irresistibly drawn by the Spirit of God. Within five months, 100,000 new converts had been added to the churches. (Five years later, 80 percent of those who had professed faith in Christ were still going on in their faith.)

The impact of the revival was felt in every nook and cranny of society.

The impact of the revival was felt in every nook and cranny of society—the gambling and alcohol businesses lost trade; taverns and brothels were closed; outstanding debts were paid; major sporting events were canceled or postponed due to lack of interest; judges were presented with white gloves because there were no cases to try; the illegitimate birth rate was reduced by 44 percent in two counties; mules in the mines had to be retrained because the coal miners no longer used profanity when giving orders.

As news of the revival spread, God began to move in other countries around the world. The United States experienced the "overflow" of what God was doing in Wales. On January 20, 1905, the headline on the front page of the *Denver Post* read: "Entire City Pauses for Prayer Even at the High Tide of Business." In Portland, Oregon, 240 department stores signed a covenant agreeing to close their doors from 11:00 a.m. to 2:00 p.m. each day while their customers and employees attended prayer meetings. In Atlantic City, ministers reported that out of a population of 50,000, only 50 adults were left unconverted.

"Do It Again, Lord!"

Few people today have ever witnessed revival and spiritual awakening on such a magnificent scale, but there is a growing sense of longing and desperation among many believers to see God "do it again"!

The God who displayed His glory in the great awakenings of the past is no less able to turn the heart of a nation today than He was 100 years ago!

We believe that the God of the Scripture, the God who displayed His glory in the great awakenings of the past, is the same God we worship today. He has not changed. He is no less able to turn the heart of a nation today than He was 100 years ago! All the social and political evils that threaten to be the undoing of our world today, all the false religions that vie for the allegiance of men—these are no match for our God. He is willing—yes, eager—to manifest Himself and His saving grace to this lost, prodigal planet. But first we must have a revived church. And a revived church consists of revived individuals.

The psalmist said, "You who seek God, let your hearts revive" (Psalm 69:32b). If you will seek Him with all your heart, you can be assured that He will restore, renew, and revive you. That revival will soon affect others. God does not lavish His goodness on us so we can simply enjoy it for ourselves. We have been saved to "proclaim the excellencies of him who called [us] out of darkness into his marvelous light" (1 Peter 2:9). One person, one family, one small group, one church—no matter how "insignificant"—that is committed to seeking the Lord can become a part of the "awakened giant" that God will use to spread His glory and the fame of His Name throughout the world.

If you will seek Him with all your heart, you can be assured that He will restore, renew, and revive you.

As you seek Him with all your heart over these next weeks, our prayer is that God will reveal Himself to you in fresh ways, that He will revive your heart, and that He will be magnified in and through your life.

Nancy Leigh DeMoss
Tim Grissom
Life Action Ministries

[1] Richard Owen Roberts, *Revival* (Wheaton: Tyndale, 1982), 20.

May God be gracious to us and bless us
and make his face to shine upon us,
that your way may be known on earth,
your saving power among all nations.
PSALM 67:1–2

HOW TO GET THE MOST FROM THIS STUDY

Seeking Him is a guide for individuals or (ideally) small groups of Christians who are committed to seeking God for revival in their lives and in our world. The book has been designed as a twelve-week study but can be adapted to a longer time frame, depending on the needs and desires of your group. Supplies needed for this study are minimal: a copy of *Seeking Him*, a Bible, and a pen or pencil. That's it.

Remember, this is an *interactive* study. While it contains much reading material, it also contains many opportunities for personal reflection and response. Feel free to mark up this book as much as you want, personalizing it with your own insights and questions.

Each lesson is divided into five daily sections for personal study. A sixth section provides a guide for group interaction. The study can be done individually without the small group component. But we believe you will find the advantages of working through this book with a group of like-minded believers to be extremely valuable. If you are not already a part of a group that is going through this study together, consider asking one or more Christian friends to join you in this journey.

In each lesson you'll find these elements:

- *Going Deeper in the Word.* Optional Bible readings for those who wish to meditate on related Scripture passages.
- *Faith-Builder Story.* An inspirational, true story of personal revival. These testimonies represent a cross-section of men, women, lay people, and vocational Christian workers. The details of their stories and the particular issues they faced may or may not be similar to yours. But the principles they learned can be applied to your life, regardless of what season or situation you may be in. This faith-building story will acquaint you with the theme of the lesson and encourage you to believe God for whatever He wants to do in your life.
- *Truth Encounter.* Studies of related Bible passages. God's Word is our guide and the Holy Spirit is our teacher. These "truth encounter" steps will help you grow in your understanding of the heart and ways of God.
- *Making It Personal.* A personal inventory exercise or series of questions for personal reflection and response. These segments will challenge you to evaluate your own behavior and attitudes, and encourage you to apply what you are learning. (Note: You may want

to photocopy certain pages from these sections for your own use, in order to have greater freedom to respond honestly to questions that are of a personal nature.)

- *Seeking Him Together.* Questions to guide group discussion and prayer time. Christianity is not a solo activity; the insights and encouragement of others are crucial to seeking God for revival. The group study time will be most valuable if all participants have read and worked through the daily homework. Each group member should commit to consistent preparation and attendance.
- *Memory Verses, Key Points, Tips, Insights,* and *Quotes.* Sidebar material that provides helpful background information, inspiring quotes, and relevant verses to memorize during the week.

This workbook is not intended to add more "shoulds" to your life. Rather, its purpose is to reveal more of God and His ways to you, to gently expose your heart, and to lead you on a pilgrimage toward greater freedom, forgiveness, fullness, and spiritual fruitfulness. You may feel as if you are unrevive-able. But take heart! Our God is a redeeming God; He is in the process of making all things new. And He promises to meet us when we seek Him with all our heart.

Lesson 1

Revival: Who Needs It?

The revival we will be talking about in this study is for God's people—those who by faith in Jesus Christ have received salvation and belong to Him. (People who do not belong to God cannot be "revived"; they first must be regenerated!) Since the days of Adam and Eve, God's people have often chosen to resist His will and rebel. Because of His great love, God keeps calling them back to intimate fellowship with Him. God's grace—the desire and power He gives us to return to Him—always accompanies His call to revival.

MEMORY VERSE

"Break up your fallow ground, for it is time to seek the Lord, til He comes and rains righteousness on you." **(Hosea 10:12, NKJV)**

2 Kings 22:8–13, 18–20
Ezra 10:1–12
Jeremiah 3:19–4:4
James 4:4–10

Day 1: **Faith-Builder Story**

1 Why did you decide to do this study? As you begin to seek God in a fresh way, what are some of your hopes? Your fears?

Read the following story of one self-made man's realization. Then answer the questions that follow.

> ***"I thought I was going to get away from the Lord! But wouldn't you know, the Spirit of God went right along with me."***

I was a man who truly had everything I ever wanted—a beautiful family, lovely home, several successful business ventures, and respect in my community and church. Like the foolish rich man in the parable Jesus told, my "barns were full and overflowing," and I felt pretty good. I certainly didn't see any need for "revival" in my life.

But God knew my true condition, and He loved me enough to do something about it. I attended an extended series of special revival services held at my church. Through the Bible teaching, God began to show me how blind and spiritually bankrupt I was. I was being confronted with truth from God's Word, and the Holy Spirit was convicting me. I found this very uncomfortable. In fact, when I had to go on a business trip for three days in the middle of the crusade, I was relieved; I thought I was going to get away from the Lord! But wouldn't you know, the Spirit of God went right along with me. Those were three miserable days of conviction.

The next Sunday morning the speaker shared the Bible story of Naaman, the commander-in-chief of the Syrian army. He was a wealthy leader who had it all together—except that he had leprosy. Naaman wanted to be healed, but he didn't want to do it God's way. So he approached it the way I would have; he loaded up six hundred shekels of gold and ten talents of silver, and went down to buy his way out of his problem. Right in the middle of this story, God's Spirit said to me, "You're just like Naaman! You've got spiritual leprosy, and you need to be healed. You can be restored, but you're going to have to do it My way."

I realized that I was proud, rebellious, ungrateful, and unyielded.

I fell on my knees and cried out to God as best I knew how, asking what He wanted me to do. In my heart I heard Him say, "I want two things: submission and obedience." Those were strange words to me, but I put myself at His mercy, confessed my sin, and repented.

God slowly showed me that I was trying to hang on to all the "things" I was accumulating instead of trusting Him to provide for us. He began to deal with me about my business and financial affairs, which resulted in a freeing, radical change of values for my family.[1]

> ***"God said, 'I want two things: submission and obedience.'"***

2 Identify some of the outer and inner factors that brought about spiritual change in this man's life.

going away on business for 3 days, God's stirring in his ♡, God's Word

3 Have you ever experienced the kind of encounter with God that he described? What was the message you needed to hear?

We are hardly the first human beings to discover our need for personal revival. Listen to the ancient cry of the psalmist's heart:

> [6] *Will you not revive us again,*
> *that your people may rejoice in you?*
> [7] *Show us your steadfast love, O Lord,*
> *and grant us your salvation.*
> [8] *Let me hear what God the Lord will speak,*
> *for he will speak peace to his people, to his saints;*
> *but let them not turn back to folly.*
> [9] *Surely his salvation is near to those who fear him,*
> *that glory may dwell in our land.* (Psalm 85:6–9)

! Key Point

Revival is for God's people who have drifted spiritually.

+ Tip

If you haven't already done so, be sure to read the Introduction on pages xii–xv. It helps define what revival is.

4 According to these verses, who needs revival?

we all do

5 What are some of the results of revival among God's people?

rejoice
God shows his stdfst love
God speaks
Salvation is near
glory dwells in their land

Day 1

Day 2: Truth Encounter

BREAKING GROUND

To begin our study let's look at the Old Testament, where we clearly see God's desire to restore His wayward people. Consider, for example, the prophet Hosea.

God sent Hosea to prophesy to the nation of Israel. Though they were God's chosen people, the nation was in a sad state of spiritual and moral decline. For years they had enjoyed God's blessings—material bounty, military strength, peaceful relations with neighboring nations—yet they still turned away from Him. They stopped viewing God as the source of their blessings and chose instead to credit themselves. They put off worshiping God. They ceased loving Him. They replaced Him with idols, worldly pursuits, and earthly wealth.

It was to these confused fellow countrymen that Hosea delivered repeated rebukes and appeals. If they did not return to the Lord, he warned, judgment would surely come. Here is the essence of Hosea's message:

> 12 *Sow for yourselves righteousness;*
> *Reap in mercy;*
> *Break up your fallow ground,*
> *For it is time to seek the Lord,*
> *Till He comes and rains righteousness on you.*
> 13 *You have plowed wickedness;*
> *You have reaped iniquity.*
> *You have eaten the fruit of lies,*
> *Because you trusted in your own way,*
> *In the multitude of your mighty men.* (Hosea 10:12–13, NKJV)

6 What was Hosea's charge against the Israelites?

Insight 

Hosea prophesied in the northern kingdom of Israel during a period of rapid moral decline ending in destruction by Assyria in 722 B.C. Hosea's family was a symbol of God's relationship with His people. His wife was a prostitute (representing spiritual adultery), and his children had prophetic names.

Key Point 

If we want to return to God, we must be prepared to break up the hard, barren ground of our spiritual lives.

Insight 

Old Testament prophets confronted sin, warned of God's judgment, and urged people to repent.

Day 2

Insight

Fallow ground—once plowed, but now lying waste—must be tilled (broken up) with a sharp plow in order to make the soil ready for seed and, ultimately, fruitful and productive.

7 What do you think it means to "break up your fallow ground"?

The condition of the Western church is remarkably similar to that of the nation of Israel. In many ways we too have forsaken God and attempted to replace Him with other gods (idols). If Hosea were preaching now, he would scarcely need to alter his words! He might tell God's people today:

- Return to your former lifestyle of righteousness, to a time when you were close to God and obeyed His Word.
- Accept God's mercy and forgive those who have wronged you.
- Allow God to "plow up" the hardened ground of your hearts, especially in those areas where you have long neglected His will.
- Grieve over your sins.
- Ponder the consequences of sin that you are experiencing.
- Accept responsibility by admitting you have brought these consequences upon yourself.
- Make seeking God your highest pursuit.

8 With the above message in mind, has there ever been a time in your life as a Christian when you walked more closely with God than you are walking right now? If yes, what are some consequences you have experienced as a result of this loss of intimacy with God?

Day 2

Day 3: Truth Encounter

GOD'S LOVE DRAWS US

Why does God want to revive our hearts and restore us to a closer relationship with Him? One major reason is that He loves us!

We need to beware of misunderstanding the heart and ways of God when we study His dealings with His people, especially in the Old Testament. Due to the numerous accounts of God's judgment recorded there, we might get the impression that God was eager to punish or that He is harsh, demanding, and impatient. But really the opposite is true. Times of judgment usually came after *years* of pleading with His people to come back to Him.

Key Point !

God's unfathomable love for us moves Him to draw us back to Him when we've strayed.

Look again at the book of Hosea. God said:

> 1 *When Israel was a child, I loved him,*
> *and out of Egypt I called my son.*
> 2 *The more they were called,*
> *the more they went away;*
> *they kept sacrificing to the Baals*
> *and burning offerings to idols.*
> 3 *Yet it was I who taught Ephraim to walk;*
> *I took them up by their arms,*
> *but they did not know that I healed them.*
> 4 *I led them with cords of kindness,*
> *with the bands of love,*
> *and I became to them as one who eases the yoke on their jaws,*
> *and I bent down to them and fed them.* (Hosea 11:1–4)

Then, after taking His people through a time of discipline and correction, God urged them once again:

> 1 *Return, O Israel, to the Lord your God,*
> *for you have stumbled because of your iniquity*
> 2 *Take with you words*
> *and return to the Lord;*
> *say to him,*
> *"Take away all iniquity;*
> *accept what is good,*
> *and we will pay with bulls*
> *the vows of our lips.*

[3] *Assyria shall not save us;*
we will not ride on horses;
and we will say no more, 'Our God'
to the work of our hands.
In you the orphan finds mercy."
[4] *I will heal their apostasy;*
I will love them freely,
for my anger has turned from them. (Hosea 14:1–4)

9 When did God start loving His people?

❍ After they "cleaned up their act."

❍ After He vented His anger on them.

❍ When they were young, at the beginning of their existence.

10 Do you think God ever stopped loving them?

❍ Yes, at least for a while.

❍ No. God always loved them, even when they needed discipline.

Explain your answer:

The passages from Hosea 11 and 14 provide "before," "during," and "after" snapshots of how and why God revives and renews His people. The constant in all three stages is His love. God loved them when they were newborns ("child" in Hosea 11:1 literally means "infant"); He loved them after they returned to Him from a season of rebellion; and He loved them throughout the whole process of correcting them.

It was His love for them, in fact, that caused them to want to return to Him. It wasn't that they suddenly "felt" love for Him again, nor that they somehow remembered how wonderful it was to live with an awareness of God's love. It was that God *caused* them to desire that love relationship again. He enabled His people to see not only how wrong they had been and why His discipline was necessary, but also that He would welcome their return because He had never ceased loving them.

Perhaps your own heart is hungering for intimacy with God—an intimacy that you haven't enjoyed for a long time or perhaps have never known. That very desire is God-initiated. He wants you back! Why? Because He loves you and knows that you cannot experience all He has for you in your present condition.

> "Revival is that strange and sovereign work of God in which He visits His own people—restoring, reanimating, and releasing them into the fullness of His blessing."
> —Stephen Olford

11 Write a prayer thanking God for His faithful love and for His desire to restore His people when they have wandered away from Him.

Day 3

Day 4: Truth Encounter

RETURNING TO OUR FIRST LOVE

The need for believers to return wholeheartedly to God—to be revived—is also addressed in the New Testament. The book of Revelation records the apostle John's vision. In this vision, Jesus speaks to seven churches. The church at Ephesus had once been a vibrant group of believers, deeply in love with Jesus. They had maintained their doctrinal purity and their separation from evil practices. They had worked hard and persevered, and they had a zeal for service. Yet something was wrong. After commending their strengths, Jesus addressed a matter of grave concern to Him:

! Key Point

We can get back our "first love" for the Lord.

> 4 *Nevertheless I have this against you, that you have left your first love.*
> 5 *Remember therefore from where you have fallen; repent and do the first works, or else I will come to you quickly and remove your lampstand from its place—unless you repent.* (Revelation 2:4–5, NKJV)

12 What had the church at Ephesus done that so displeased the Lord? Put into your own words what it means to leave "your first love."

13 What three verbs do you note in Jesus' command? What light does this shed on the process of revival?

Day 4

Over the years, the Christians at Ephesus had somehow lost sight of the Savior. Their love for Him had lost its fervor. They had transferred their affection elsewhere, and this deviation threatened to cost them dearly.

God wants us to love Him first and foremost. When we find ourselves trusting in people instead of the Lord, this indicates that our heart's focus has shifted from Him (Jeremiah 17:5). Love for people—friends, family members, or even ourselves—can compete with our love for Him (Matthew 10:37). Other substitutes for a God-centered love relationship may include money, pleasure, friends, work, ritual in worship, the teachings of respected leaders, or Bible knowledge without a relationship with Christ.

Revival does not begin when a struggling, wayward person decides to return to the Lord but rather when the loving heavenly Father, wanting His people to enjoy the safety and security of His love, calls him or her back to Himself. God is the initiator; the call to revival is a plea of love from the heart of God.

Insight 

A major city in western Asia Minor (now Turkey), Ephesus was a center of early Christianity. Paul based his operations there for three years, and the apostle John is believed to have spent his final years as bishop of Ephesus.

14 Have you transferred your love for God to some other place? What are some things that may be competing with your love for Him?

Day 4

Day5: Making It Personal

Revival is the sovereign work of God. He chooses when and to whom He sends it. It is also true, however, that there are things we can do to prepare for revival in our lives. Being prepared for what God has determined to do is a pattern we see throughout Scripture. For example, on the eve of their passage into the Promised Land, Joshua charged the children of Israel, "Consecrate yourselves, for tomorrow the Lord will do wonders among you" (Joshua 3:5). In the same way, we can prepare our hearts for spiritual renewal.

> "As long as we are content to live without revival, we will."
>
> —Leonard Ravenhill

The following questions are designed to reveal specific areas of which to be aware as you prepare for personal (as well as corporate) revival. They are not meant to be guilt-producers, just a helpful tool. Answer each question as honestly as possible—not as it once was in your life or as others think of you, but based on what God reveals to be the current condition of your heart.

Read the Bible passages if time allows. Agree with God about each need He reveals. Confess each sin that He exposes. Praise Him for His awesome love and power to forgive. Don't be in a hurry; give God time to speak and give yourself time to respond.

Before you begin working through the checklist, pray the prayer of Psalm 139:23–24: "Search me,O God, and know my heart! Try me and know my thoughts! And see if there be any grievous way in me, and lead me in the way everlasting!"

Preparing My Heart for Revival

1. Genuine Salvation (2 Corinthians 5:17)

a. Was there a time in my life when I genuinely repented of (was aware of and turned away from) my sin?

b. Was there a time in my life when I placed all my trust in Jesus Christ alone to save me?

c. Was there ever a time in my life when I completely surrendered to Jesus Christ as the Master and Lord of my life?

2. God's Word (Psalm 119:97, 140)

a. Do I love to read and meditate on the Word of God?

b. Are my personal devotions consistent and meaningful?

c. Do I apply God's Word to my everyday life?

3. Humility (Isaiah 57:15)
    a. Am I quick to recognize and agree with God in confession when I have sinned?
    b. Am I quick to admit to others when I am wrong?
    c. Do I rejoice when others are praised and recognized and my accomplishments go unnoticed by people?

4. Obedience (1 Samuel 15:22; Hebrews 13:17)
    a. Do I consistently obey what I know God wants me to do?
    b. Do I consistently obey the human authorities God has placed over my life?

5. Pure Heart (1 John 1:9)
    a. Do I confess my sin by name?
    b. Do I keep "short sin accounts" with God (confess and forsake as He convicts)?
    c. Am I willing to give up all sin for God?

6. Clear Conscience (Acts 24:16)
    a. Do I consistently seek forgiveness from those I wrong or offend?
    b. Is my conscience clear with every person? (Can I honestly say, "There is no one I have ever wronged or offended in any way and not gone back to that person and sought his forgiveness and made it right"?)

7. Priorities (Matthew 6:33)
    a. Does my schedule reveal that God is first in my life?
    b. Does my checkbook reveal that God is first in my life?

"Revival awakens in our hearts an increased awareness of the presence of God, a new love for God, a new hatred for sin, and a hunger for His Word."
—Del Fehsenfeld Jr.

8. Values (Colossians 3:12)
   a. Do I love what God loves and hate what God hates?
   b. Do I value highly the things that please God (for example: giving, witnessing to lost souls, studying His Word, praying)?
   c. Are my affections and goals fixed on eternal values?

9. Sacrifice (Philippians 3:7–8)
   a. Am I willing to sacrifice whatever is necessary to see God move in my life and church (time, convenience, comfort, reputation, pleasure, and so on)?
   b. Is my life characterized by genuine sacrifice for the cause of Christ?

10. Spirit Control (Galatians 5:22–25; Ephesians 5:18–21)
   a. Am I allowing Jesus to be Lord of every area of my life?
   b. Am I allowing the Holy Spirit to "fill" (control) my life each day?
   c. Is there consistent evidence of the "fruit of the Spirit" being produced in my life?

11. "First Love" (Philippians 1:21, 23)
   a. Am I as much in love with Jesus as I have ever been?
   b. Am I devoted to Jesus, filled with His joy and peace, and making Him the continual object of my affection?

12. Motives (Matthew 10:28; Acts 5:29)
   a. Am I more concerned with what God thinks about my life than with what others think?
   b. Would I pray, read my Bible, give, and serve as much if nobody but God ever noticed?
   c. Am I more concerned about pleasing God than I am about being accepted and appreciated by others?

13. Moral Purity (Ephesians 5:3–4)

   a. Do I keep my mind free from books, magazines, or entertainment that could stimulate fantasizing or thoughts that are not morally pure?

   b. Are my conversation and behavior pure and above reproach?

14. Forgiveness (Colossians 3:12–13)

   a. Do I seek to resolve conflicts in relationships as soon as possible?

   b. Am I quick to forgive those who wrong or hurt me?

15. Evangelism (Luke 24:47–48; Romans 9:3)

   a. Do I have a burden for lost souls?

   b. Do I consistently witness for Christ?

16. Prayer (1 Timothy 2:1)

   a. Am I faithful in praying for the needs of others?

   b. Do I pray specifically, fervently, and faithfully for revival in my life, my church, and our nation?

"Revival is not some emotion or worked up excitement; it is rather an invasion from heaven which brings to man a conscious awareness of God."

—Stephen Olford

---

[1] The Faith-Builder story in Lesson 1 is adapted from "Transformed by His Grace," *Spirit of Revival*, vol. 25, no. 1, March 1995, pp. 15-16, published by Life Action Ministries.

Day 5

Seeking Him Together

Use these questions and activities each week for group discussion of the material each member has completed during the week. Remember that all responses need to be respected and held in confidence. The point of meeting together is to learn from one another and to encourage each other to seek God more fully.

Opening It Up

1. Why have you chosen to participate in this study on seeking God and personal revival?

Talking It Over

2. Before beginning this study guide, what did you think "revival" was? How has your view of revival changed thus far?

3. If you read the passages in "Going Deeper in the Word," what parts encouraged you? What, if any, questions did they raise?

4. What did you learn from the Faith-Builder story of the self-made man? What things do you tend to hold on to for security, even though they could be easily taken away?

5. The prophet Hosea was sent to the nation of Israel. They had turned away from God and replaced Him with other things. What are some ways that Christians today replace God with other things?

6. Read Hosea 10:12–13 aloud. Review the seven-point summary of Hosea's message on page 6. If you're willing, explain to the group how one point of the sermon applies to you personally.

Return to righteousness; Reap love; Allow God to plow; Grieve over sins, Ponder sins; Make seeking God highest pursuit..

Tip +

Do not hastily pass over this Scripture or the summary points. Allow God to speak to your heart. Listen and respond as the Holy Spirit examines you.

7. Tell the group about someone you know or have heard about who has unselfishly loved another person, even though that person was not worthy of it. How does this real-life example help you understand God's love for His wayward children?

Revival causes us to want to read his word

8. What does the idea that God initiates revival in His people tell you about God? What does it tell you about yourself?

Seeking Him **Together**

9. "Preparing My Heart for Revival" (Day 5) was a spiritual diagnostic tool provided to help assess your own need for personal revival. If you feel comfortable, share a specific way that God used this exercise to bring conviction or to reveal an area of need in your life.

"Revival is not just an emotional touch; it is a complete takeover!"

—A Newly Revived Believer

Praying for Revival

There are countless joys and rewards of walking closely with and seeking God. Below are eight specific benefits or results of personal revival. Have one person or several people read these aloud.

1. **Revival restores first love.** In times of revival, the love we once had for God is rekindled.

2. **Revival rebuilds a desire for God's Word, prayer, praise, and obedience.** As we experience greater intimacy with God, those spiritual disciplines and activities that we once dreaded become a delight.

3. **Revival resolves conflicts.** God's grace enables us to humble ourselves, admit our sinful attitudes, forgive those who have hurt us, and seek the forgiveness of those we have offended. Reconciliation—with God and others—is a mark of true revival.

4. **Revival repairs broken marriages.** Do you know any "hopeless" family situations, such as couples on the brink of divorce or perhaps deeply embittered toward one another yet staying together for the sake of appearance? When real revival comes, *no situation* is hopeless.

5. **Revival removes bitterness, fear, and worry.** "We have seen more take place in her life in four days than we have in four years of counseling." This is how a father and mother described the drastic change in their formerly rebellious and immoral teenage daughter. As often happens in revival, this young woman came under deep conviction over feelings of bitterness that she held toward someone. The reasons for her rebellious behavior became obvious as she began honestly to admit her hurts and accept responsibility for her wrong responses and actions. Anger and bitterness soon lost their grip, and she was set free.

6. **Revival refreshes the spirit**. Do you live with nearly constant pressure and anxiety? Have you discovered that the things you tend to turn to for relief neither satisfy you nor remove the stress? According to Acts 3:20, "Times of refreshing" come from "the presence of the Lord." What an apt description of revival! God invites us to come to His presence. There—and only there—will we find genuine rest.

7. **Revival renews the mind.** A revived life is marked by God-centered thinking. We begin to view things from His perspective rather than from our own limited and natural vantage point.

8. **Revival reforms the life.** Someone has described revival as a "complete takeover" in which God is returned to His rightful place as Lord of our lives. Old habits are put away, and new ones are established. Resentment and despair are buried and replaced with contentment and hope. Forgiveness flows freely.

Which result(s) of revival do you particularly need and desire to see in your own life?

Break into groups of no more than four or five individuals and take time to pray for each other in one or more of these areas:

- **PRAY** that Jesus Christ will become the first love in each heart.
- **PRAY** that you will have an increased desire to read and obey God's Word and to worship Him.
- **PRAY** that any outstanding conflicts would be resolved.
- **PRAY** that any family conflicts represented in your group will be reconciled.
- **PRAY** that you would be set free from any bitterness, anger, and worry, and that each life would be characterized by love, forgiveness, and God-centered trust.
- **PRAY** that each one will cultivate a habit of turning to God *first* when faced with any kind of trial.
- **PRAY** that God will renew your mind.
- **PRAY** that each member of your group would experience true revival as you "Seek Him" together in the days ahead.

Lesson 2

Humility: Coming to God on His Terms

Humility is a virtue more often praised than sought. Who wants to think little of himself? The world admires the self-confident, the ambitious, yes, even the proud! Yet biblical humility—recognizing oneself as a sinner before the holy God—is a prerequisite for starting down the path to revival.

MEMORY VERSE

"For everyone who exalts himself will be humbled, and he who humbles himself will be exalted." **(Luke 14:11)**

Going Deeper in the Word

Psalm 8
Proverbs 8:13; 11:2; 16:18; 29:23
Micah 6:6–8
Luke 18:9–14
John 13:1–17

Day 1: Faith-Builder Story

1 Have you ever known someone who was truly humble? How did humility evidence itself in his/her life?

Read the following story and answer the question that follows.

> I was a demanding husband and father. I was convinced that I was in good spiritual condition but felt that my family members had significant spiritual needs. I think the reason their "problems" bothered me was because they made me look bad. After all, I was well known in the community and served as a deacon in our church—I wanted my family to make me look good.
>
> Needless to say, I had a real problem with pride!
>
> Revival began in my life with my getting honest with God. He began to quietly work on me. I'd been having trouble sleeping, and one night I was awake all night thinking about something I'd done several years earlier and had tried to forget. God was urging me to deal with this—something I considered a "closed case." I knew that if I did what God was prompting me to do, I would risk going to prison.
>
> I had been called as a witness in a federal court trial. Disturbed by the less than honorable motives of one of the parties involved, I determined that it was up to me to see that things "came out right." Therefore, I purposely gave vague answers to direct questions. I did not tell "the whole truth" as I had sworn to do. So here I was, awake during the middle of the night, trying to reason with God that it was best to let bygones be bygones. It was too late. What good would it do?
>
> But God didn't agree! No matter what other areas of my life I surrendered or what deep sin struggles I confessed, this was the specific issue that God wanted to address. Finally I said, "Yes, Lord." I called the judge's office and explained my situation to his assistant. I told her that I had been dishonest on the witness stand and that God had impressed on me the need to make it right. I was prepared to do whatever the law required or receive whatever punishment was due me.
>
> I didn't hear back from the judge for seven months. That's a long time

to wait when you think you might be going to prison! But it was all a part of God's cleansing process. Finally they called me to appear for a deposition, in which I would be questioned by attorneys from both sides. When I finally heard the outcome of that meeting, after waiting an additional five months, I was informed that neither side wished to reopen the case. I was a free man! Then again, my real freedom had come the year before when God first began to move in my life.

It hasn't all been blissful, but many things in my life and family have changed as God continues to peel away the layers of pride and disobedience. My family now seems to want my leadership—a real change from my demanding it. The weaknesses and needs in others aren't so bothersome to me. I feel a new compassion and patience toward people, now that I have faced the skeletons in my own closet. And I can sleep through the night.

"[Seven months] is a long time to wait when you think you might be going to prison!"

"God continues to peel away the layers of pride and disobedience."

2 What evidence of pride do you see in this man's life? What evidence of humility?

In preparation for revival, God convicts His people of their sin and calls them to return to Him. A familiar passage from the Old Testament outlines how we must respond to God if we wish to experience the revival He desires to send.

> *If My people who are called by My name will humble themselves, and pray and seek My face, and turn from their wicked ways, then I will hear from heaven, and will forgive their sin and heal their land.* (2 Chronicles 7:14, NKJV)

3 List the four conditions God sets forth for His people in this Scripture passage.

Insight 

In its immediate context,this passage in 2 Chronicles 7 is directed to the nation of Israel. However, the principles it reveals have a timeless application to every believer.

4 What is the first of the four conditions in 2 Chronicles 7:14? Why do you think God put this one first?

Day 1

Day 2: Truth Encounter

GOD'S VIEW OF PRIDE

Pride, the opposite of humility, is the most formidable roadblock to revival. Pride blinds us to our true spiritual condition and causes us to think more highly of ourselves than we should. When we are proud, self becomes more important than anyone else. When we are proud, we are driven to promote ourselves and to protect our reputation. Pride keeps us at a distance from God.

Key Point 

Pride is a roadblock to revival.

5 What do the following verses reveal about pride? How does it manifest itself? How does God view it? What are the consequences of having a proud heart?

Psalm 10:4 ____________
Psalm 31:23 ____________
Proverbs 8:13 ____________
Proverbs 11:2 ____________
Proverbs 16:18 ____________
Proverbs 29:23 ____________
Obadiah 1:3 ____________
Matthew 23:12 ____________
James 4:6 ____________

6 Pride is obviously not a casual issue with God. Why do you think God is so opposed to human pride?

____
____
____
____

"The essential vice, the utmost evil, is Pride. Unchastity, greed, drunkenness, and all that, are mere flea-bites in comparison: it was through Pride that the devil became the devil. Pride leads to every other vice: it is the complete anti-God state of mind."

—C. S. Lewis

As strongly as God is repulsed by pride, He is drawn to humility, as this verse shows.

For thus says the One who is high and lifted up,
who inhabits eternity, whose name is Holy:
"I dwell in the high and holy place,
and also with him who is of a contrite and lowly spirit,
to revive the spirit of the lowly,
and to revive the heart of the contrite." (Isaiah 57:15)

7 What do you think it means to have a "contrite and lowly spirit"?

8 According to this passage, how does God respond to those who are truly humble?

God chooses to exalt the humble. He promises to live in intimate fellowship with them. Those with humble hearts are candidates for revival.

9 Write a prayer expressing your response to what you have seen in God's Word today about pride and humility.

Day2

Day 3: **Truth Encounter**

TWO KINGS, TWO CHOICES

The inclination of our hearts toward pride or humility becomes evident when God brings to our attention something in our lives that is not pleasing to Him. The way we respond to Him in moments of conviction reveals the true condition of our heart. This is illustrated in the lives of two Old Testament kings, Rehoboam and Asa.

Rehoboam inherited the throne of Israel from his father, Solomon. In the midst of his reign, Rehoboam encountered trouble.

> [1]*When the rule of Rehoboam was established and he was strong, he*
> *abandoned the law of the Lord, and all Israel with him.* [2]*In the fifth*
> *year of King Rehoboam, because they had been unfaithful to the Lord,*
> *Shishak king of Egypt came up against Jerusalem* [3]*with 1,200 chariots*
> *and 60,000 horsemen....* [4]*And he took the fortified cities of Judah and*
> *came as far as Jerusalem.*
>
> [5]*Then Shemaiah the prophet came to Rehoboam and to the princes of Judah, who had gathered at Jerusalem because of Shishak, and said to them, "Thus says the Lord, 'You abandoned me, so I have abandoned you to the hand of Shishak.'"* (2 Chronicles 12:1–5)

Rehoboam's heart was filled with sin and self. He had led the nation far away from God. The Lord raised up an enemy to punish Rehoboam for his rebellion. God wanted Rehoboam to understand why the nation was under siege, so He sent a prophet to explain. Read what happened next.

> [6]*Then the princes of Israel and the king humbled themselves and said,*
> *"The Lord is righteous."* [7]*When the Lord saw that they humbled themselves, the word of the Lord came to Shemaiah: "They have humbled themselves. I will not destroy them, but I will grant them some deliverance, and my wrath shall not be poured out on Jerusalem by the hand of Shishak."* (2 Chronicles 12:6–7)

10 How did Rehoboam and the leaders of the people respond when they were confronted with their sin?

____

____

____

____

Key Point 

The way we respond when we are confronted with our sin reveals the condition of our heart.

Insight 

Pharaoh Shishak invaded Judah around 926 BC, plundering Jerusalem and forcing Rehoboam to pay tribute money. The Egyptian version of this invasion lists the names of more than 100 cities that Shishak ("Sheshonk" in Egyptian) claimed to have captured. But Jerusalem was not destroyed, and Judah retained its nationhood.

11 How did God respond when His people humbled themselves? How did the whole nation benefit from Rehoboam's humility?

Now look at Rehoboam's grandson, Asa, who became king of Judah three years after Rehoboam's death. Asa had a long and (for the most part) prosperous reign. The Bible records many positive things about Asa and his leadership. He began his reign by taking some major steps of obedience.

> *2And Asa did what was good and right in the eyes of the Lord his God.
> 3He took away the foreign altars and the high places and broke down
> the pillars and cut down the Asherim 4and commanded Judah to seek
> the Lord, the God of their fathers, and to keep the law and the commandment. 5He also took out of all the cities of Judah the high places
> and the incense altars. And the kingdom had rest under him. 6He built
> fortified cities in Judah, for the land had rest. He had no war in those
> years, for the Lord gave him peace…. 7So they built and prospered.*
> (2 Chronicles 14:2–7)

Insight

The Israelites repeatedly gave in to the temptation of adopting Canaanite worship. Pillars were used in Canaanite worship to represent the male god Baal, and wooden poles were set up to represent the goddess Asherah. "High places" were stone platforms where pagan rituals were conducted. Incense was used in such worship.

Even under Asa's godly leadership, however, trouble eventually came to his kingdom. The Ethiopian army drew up for battle against Judah. In his time of trouble, Asa trusted in the Lord. He cried out to God and, by His hand, routed the enemy. God honored Asa for his faith and affirmed His blessing on his leadership. Asa responded in humility, and the spiritual resolve of the nation was deepened (see 2 Chronicles 15).

Several years later another enemy approached, and this time Asa responded differently. Rather than trusting in the Lord, Asa turned to the nearby Syrians for help. God sent a prophet to rebuke him for this folly.

[7]At that time Hanani the seer came to Asa king of Judah and said to him, "Because you relied on the king of Syria, and did not rely on the Lord your God, the army of the king of Syria has escaped you. [8]Were not the Ethiopians and the Libyans a huge army with very many chariots and horsemen? Yet because you relied on the Lord, he gave them into your hand.

[9]"For the eyes of the Lord run to and fro throughout the whole earth, to give strong support to those whose heart is blameless toward him. You have done foolishly in this, for from now on you will have wars." (2 Chronicles 16:7–9)

12 Why was it wrong for Asa to look to the Syrians for help against his enemies?

Even though he had erred greatly, Asa was given the opportunity to humble himself, acknowledge his wrongdoing, and receive God's mercy. The Scripture goes on to tell us how he responded to the prophet from God:

[10]Then Asa was angry with the seer and put him in the stocks in prison, for he was in a rage with him because of this. And Asa inflicted cruelties upon some of the people at the same time.… [12]In the thirty-ninth year of his reign Asa was diseased in his feet, and his disease became severe. Yet even in his disease he did not seek the Lord, but sought help from physicians. [13]And Asa slept with his fathers, dying in the forty-first year of his reign. (2 Chronicles 16:10, 12–13)

"Oh! man, hate pride, flee from it, abhor it, do not let it dwell with you!"
—C. H. Spurgeon

13 What evidences of pride do you see in this account? How did Asa's pride affect his responses and his leadership?

14 Rehoboam and Asa stand as contrasting illustrations of humility and pride.

Which king began his reign in pride and rebellion? ____________

Which king ended his reign in pride and rebellion? ____________

Both men sinned. Both were confronted with their sin. One accepted this rebuke as God's way of cleansing; the other received it as an assault on his reputation. Humility restored Rehoboam; pride ruined Asa.

15 How do you typically respond when God uses others to point out areas of sin or failure in your life? Is your response more like that of Rehoboam or Asa?

____

____

____

____

Day3

Day 4: **Truth Encounter**

HUMILITY IS NECESSARY

Humility has never been popular in the eyes of the world. If you want to get ahead, self-confidence and self-promotion are the fail-proof prescriptions for success. However, in the kingdom of God, and especially in the process of revival, humility and brokenness are essential.

Humbling ourselves is the first step we take toward God. But how do we do this? Isaiah provides some instruction from his personal experience.

> 1In the year that King Uzziah died I saw the Lord sitting upon a throne,
> high and lifted up; and the train of his robe filled the temple. 2Above
> him stood the seraphim. Each had six wings: with two he covered his
> face, and with two he covered his feet, and with two he flew. 3And one
> called to another and said:
>
> *"Holy, holy, holy is the Lord of hosts;*
> *the whole earth is full of his glory!"*
>
> 4And the foundations of the thresholds shook at the voice of him who
> called, and the house was filled with smoke. 5And I said: "Woe is me!
> For I am lost; for I am a man of unclean lips, and I dwell in the midst of
> a people of unclean lips; for my eyes have seen the King, the Lord of
> hosts!"
>
> 6Then one of the seraphim flew to me, having in his hand a burning
> coal that he had taken with tongs from the altar. 7And he touched my
> mouth and said: "Behold, this has touched your lips; your guilt is taken
> away, and your sin atoned for." (Isaiah 6:1–7)

16 Number the events in the order in which they occurred:

Isaiah saw the Lord in His awesome holiness and majesty.

Isaiah confessed his sin.

God forgave and cleansed Isaiah.

Isaiah recognized the depth of his own sinfulness and was overwhelmed.

Insight

King Uzziah died in 740 BC. That death marked a turning point as this good king was ultimately succeeded by the wicked King Ahaz, who led the nation toward destruction.

Key Point 

An awareness of God's holiness drives us to acknowledge our sin and receive God's forgiveness.

"They that know God will be humble; they that know themselves cannot be proud."

—John Flavel

17 What do you learn about personal revival from Isaiah's experience?

Isaiah's vision of God in the temple provides an illustration of the process of revival. Like Isaiah, when we are brought to a new awareness of God's holiness, we recognize the depth of our own sinfulness. With a broken, contrite heart, we confess and forsake our sin. God responds to our humility with forgiveness; He restores us and makes us usable instruments to fulfill His purposes in our world.

18 The transformation in Isaiah's life began with a vision of God. How does knowing God and "seeing" His glory and holiness change our lives? What can we do to gain a clearer perspective of God as He really is?

Day 4

Day 5: Making It Personal

"The sacrifices of God are a broken spirit; a broken and a contrite heart, O God, you will not despise" (Psalm 51:17). The following list contrasts the heart of a proud person with the heart of a humble and contrite person.

Ask God to show you which characteristics of a proud heart are true of you. Circle the number next to each of those items in the left hand column.

Proud people...	Humble people...
1. focus on the failures of others	1. are overwhelmed with a sense of their own spiritual need
2. have a critical, fault-finding spirit; look at everyone else's faults with a microscope but their own with a telescope	2. are compassionate; can forgive much because they know how much they have been forgiven
3. are self-righteous; look down on others	3. esteem all others better than themselves
4. have an independent, self-sufficient spirit	4. have a dependent spirit; recognize their need for others
5. have to prove they are right	5. are not argumentative
6. claim rights; have a demanding spirit	6. yield their rights; have a meek spirit
7. are self-protective of their time, their rights, and their reputation	7. are self-denying
8. desire to be served	8. are motivated to serve others
9. desire to make a name for themselves	9. are motivated to be faithful and to make others a success
10. desire self-advancement	10. desire to promote others
11. have a drive to be recognized and appreciated	11. have a sense of their own unworthiness; are thrilled that God would use them at all
12. are wounded when others are promoted and they are overlooked	12. are eager for others to get the credit and rejoice when others are lifted up

"If anyone would like to acquire humility, I can, I think, tell him the first step. The first step is to realize that one is proud.... If you think you're not conceited, it means you are very conceited indeed."

—C. S. Lewis

13. have a subconscious feeling that says, "This organization is privileged to have me and my gifts"; think of what they can do for God	13. have a heart attitude that says, "I don't deserve to have any part in this work"; know that they have nothing to offer God except what He enables them to do
14. feel confident in how much they know	14. are humbled by how very much they have to learn
15. are self-conscious	15. are not concerned with self at all
16. keep others at arms' length	16. are willing to risk getting close to others and to take risks of loving intimately
17. are quick to blame others	17. accept personal responsibility and can see where they are wrong in a situation
18. are unapproachable or defensive when criticized	18. receive criticism with a humble, open spirit
19. are overly concerned with what others think; work to protect their own image and reputation	19. are concerned with being real; what matters to them is not what others think but what God knows; are willing to risk their own reputation
20. find it difficult to share their spiritual needs with others	20. are willing to be open and transparent with others as God directs
21. want to be sure that no one finds out when they have sinned; have instinct to cover up	21. once broken, don't care who knows or who finds out; are willing to be exposed because they have nothing to lose
22. have a hard time saying, "I was wrong; will you please forgive me?"	22. are quick to admit failure and to seek forgiveness when necessary
23. tend to deal in generalities when confessing sin	23. are able to acknowledge specifics when confessing their sin
24. are concerned about the consequences of their sin	24. are grieved over the cause, the root of their sin

"A truly humble man is sensible of his natural distance from God; of his dependence on Him; of the insufficiency of his own power and wisdom."

—Jonathan Edwards

Day 5

25. are remorseful over their sin, sorry that they got found out or caught	25. are truly repentant over their sin; forsake their sin
26. wait for the other to come and ask forgiveness when there is a misunderstanding or conflict in a relationship	26. take the initiative to be reconciled when there is a misunderstanding or a conflict in relationships, no matter how wrong the other may have been
27. compare themselves with others and feel worthy of honor	27. compare themselves to the holiness of God and feel desperate need for His mercy
28. are blind to their true heart condition	28. walk in the light
29. don't think they have anything to repent of	29. realize they have need of a continual heart attitude of repentance
30. don't think they need revival but are sure that everyone else does	30. continually sense their need for a fresh encounter with God and for a fresh filling of His Holy Spirit[1]

"I am persuaded that love and humility are the highest attainments in the school of Christ and the brightest evidences that He is indeed our Master."

—John Newton

So what is your pride quotient? We should not wait for God to humble us. God says we must *humble ourselves.* When we do, God is always there with open arms of grace and love. Respond now to God in prayer.

- Agree with Him about each evidence of pride that He has shown you through this exercise.
- Ask His forgiveness for your pride, realizing that pride is really an attempt to be "as God."
- Ask Him to continue to reveal anything that indicates pride in your life.
- Ask Him to show you any practical steps you could take to humble yourself before Him and others.

[1] The "Proud/Humble" list in Lesson 2 is adapted from a message given by Nancy Leigh DeMoss, © 1995. Used by permission. To order a bookmark with the complete list, write: Revive Our Hearts, P.O. Box 2000, Niles, MI 49120 or visit ReviveOurHearts.com or email: info@ReviveOurHearts.com.

Seeking Him **Together**

Opening It Up

1. To review,

- Who is revival for?
- Why does God revive His people?
- Who initiates revival—us or God?

Talking It Over

> "It is pride that is at the root of all other sins: envy, contention, discontent, and all hindrances that would prevent renewal."
>
> —Richard Baxter

2. The man in this week's story said that personal revival did not come in his life until he humbled himself before God and others. Why do you think humility—toward God and toward others—is vital to revival? How does pride hinder revival?

3. Why do you think the man's family responded better to his leadership after he had obeyed God?

4. Our Bible study compared two kings, Rehoboam and Asa. What did you learn from each king's response to God's Word in their lives?

5. What are some ways that pride is manifested in our lives? How does it affect our relationships with other people?

6. Read 1 Peter 5:5–7 aloud and discuss the following questions:

What does it mean to be "clothed with humility" toward one another?

How might our homes, workplaces, and churches be different if believers were all "clothed with humility"?

What are some ways God opposes the proud?

How does God respond to humility?

Seeking Him Together

How are worry and anxiety expressions of pride rather than humility?

"Humility is the displacement of self and the enthronement of Christ. Humility means Christ is all and self is nothing."

—T. A. Hegre

7. Isaiah had a life-changing encounter with God when he saw who God was (see Isaiah 6). How can we come to "see" and know God as He really is?

8. What means has God used to convict you of sin within the past few months? How did you respond?

9. How did God speak to you as you went through the list of "proud versus humble" people?

10. If you feel comfortable, share one expression of pride you have been convicted of in this past week. (The willingness to share an answer with the group may be one practical way for you to humble yourself before the Lord!)

Praying for Revival

In closing, pray together for God's continued grace to seek Him with humility. Ask for His mercy in your individual lives and in His church. Confess specific evidences of pride that you still battle in your lives. Ask God to make you more sensitive to the manifestations of pride in your own life. Pray for a "baptism of humility" in the body of Christ—among lay people and Christian leaders. Ask God to reveal His awesome greatness in such a way that all will bow before Him.

Optional 

During the next week, set aside some time to meditate on the holiness of God. You may want to read specific Scriptures and sing hymns or choruses that emphasize His awesome holiness. When we focus on how great and holy God is, we realize how small and sinful we are by comparison.

Lesson 3

Honesty: Silence Is Not Always Golden

Seeking God for personal revival requires a level of honesty that, at first, may seem quite threatening. Covering up our faults and failures is an involuntary reflex. At first glance, it often seems like the best option. We want others to think the best of us. However, humility—one of the first prerequisites for revival—requires the willingness to be honest with God and others about our true spiritual condition.

MEMORY VERSE

"Whoever conceals his transgressions will not prosper, but he who confesses and forsakes them will obtain mercy." (Proverbs 28:13)

Going Deeper in the Word

Genesis 3:6–13
Proverbs 30:7–9
Acts 5:1–11

Day 1: **Faith-Builder Story**

1 Think about a time when you were tempted to leave a better impression of yourself than was true.What did you do? Why?

Read this story about one man's difficult journey to "walk into the light" with God, with his wife, and with others. Then answer the questions.

> If you're from my generation, you may remember the song "The Great Pretender." Buck Ram wrote it. The Platters sang it. But to my great shame, I personified it.
>
> In January of 1995, my wife and I were at the end of our rope. Our marriage had disintegrated to the point where reconciliation seemed hopeless. We had been to counselor after counselor, and nothing seemed to help.
>
> All the while I was pastoring a growing metropolitan church. I had a good reputation in our state denominational association and was often called upon for speaking engagements. Outwardly, I was happy and successful. Inwardly, I was in turmoil. My wife and I were emotionally divorced and were living in opposite ends of our home.

"Many times on Sunday mornings we'd be screaming at one another, and five mintues later [I would] enter the pulpit to preach."

> For eight months my wife had been unable to attend church because the pastor, her husband, was such a hypocrite. Many times on Sunday mornings we'd be screaming at one another and slamming doors. I would get in my car, drive to church, and five minutes later enter the pulpit to preach and pretend. I knew that a man has no ministry if he doesn't have a ministry at home, but I refused to realize that it applied to me.
>
> The time came to have a scheduled revival crusade at our church. I knew I had to call the revival team and tell them what was going on. They suggested that my wife and I first attend a crusade in another city. This way we would be forced to concentrate on our marriage and personal needs. So we traveled to the conference, where we checked into separate hotel rooms. During the first session, we sat together miserably. Finally, she said,"I haven't sat with you in church for eight months, and I can't do it now." So she went to the back of the auditorium.

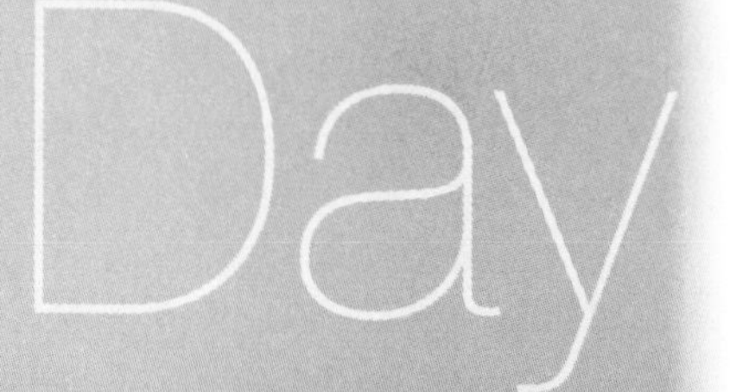

On Monday we each met with one of the team leaders. He wasn't impressed with my credentials or church reputation and wasn't interested in protecting it. In a loving and penetrating way, he simply began to confront me with truth.

We didn't talk about my wife; we talked about me. I was finally forced to face the reality that I had denied for so long. I was challenged to list the ways I had wounded my wife's spirit. After the thirty-first entry, I was overwhelmed, and I knew the list still wasn't complete! But the journey of honesty had begun, and so had the journey of reconciliation and healing. In prayer before the Lord, I dealt with the issues I had listed. Then I confessed them to my wife.

Of the many ways that I had hurt her, one in particular brought great conviction. Some of our congregants knew that she had had emotional struggles when we returned from the mission field years earlier. Both by my silence and by some of the things I had said, I had led my congregation to believe that she was the problem and I was a helpless victim. That was hypocrisy in the highest degree because I was the real problem.

"We went straight to our bedroom and got our wedding rings out. They had been put away for a long time."

As I confessed my many failures and sought my wife's forgiveness, God began to soften her heart. I discovered that a wife has a vast reservoir of patience and understanding if she knows that her husband is willing to take personal responsibility and to be honest about his needs and struggles.When we got home, we went straight to our bedroom and got our wedding rings out (they had been put away for a long time) and committed to begin rebuilding our marriage.[1]

2 How had this man deceived himself, his wife, and others? What were the consequences?

3 Why is it so difficult to be transparent about our failures and needs with those we are the closest to?

Read the following verses from the book of Psalms:

[1]Lord, who shall sojourn in your tent?
Who shall dwell on your holy hill?
[2]He who walks blamelessly and does what is right
and speaks truth in his heart. (Psalm 15:1–2)

[3]Who shall ascend the hill of the Lord?
And who shall stand in his holy place?
[4]He who has clean hands and a pure heart,
who does not lift up his soul to what is false
and does not swear deceitfully.
[5]He will receive blessing from the Lord
and righteousness from the God of his salvation.
(Psalm 24:3–5)

4 What do you think it means to speak truth in your heart? Why do you think complete honesty with God and others is a prerequisite to enjoying an intimate relationship with God?

Day 2: Truth Encounter

HONEST TO GOD

Ever since Adam and Eve first disobeyed God, the tendency to cover our sin has been a part of our sinful human nature (see Genesis 3:7–8). We don't have to be trained how to hide or pretend—it comes naturally. Even after we are redeemed in Christ and the Holy Spirit takes up residence within us, we often battle the urge to deceive. But God cannot bless or revive a heart that refuses to acknowledge the truth.

Yesterday we read two passages from the Psalms in which David expressed the importance of walking before God in truth. This was a lesson David learned the hard way.

Though handpicked by God to be a leader, David rejected God's law and committed the heinous sin of adultery (see 2 Samuel 11). As damaging as that was, however, he could have spared his household and his kingdom many months of anguish had he simply been honest about his failure. Instead, he chose to hide, cover up, and deny his wrongdoing.

He lied to Bathsheba, the woman with whom he had committed adultery. He lied to her husband, Uriah. He lied to his warriors. He lived a lie before his people. He lied to himself by acting as if what he'd done really wasn't all that bad, that he could get away with it, and that there would be no major consequence to suffer.

Above all, David lied to God by attempting to cover his sin and refusing to acknowledge and confess it.

Psalm 32 is David's firsthand account of the process he went through to discover the profound joy of experiencing God's mercy and forgiveness. Read this passage and then respond to the questions that follow.

> 1 *Blessed is the one whose transgression is forgiven,*
> *whose sin is covered.*
> 2 *Blessed is the man against whom the Lord counts no iniquity,*
> *and in whose spirit there is no deceit.*
> 3 *For when I kept silent, my bones wasted away*
> *through my groaning all day long.*
> 4 *For day and night your hand was heavy upon me;*
> *my strength was dried up as by the heat of summer.* Selah
> 5 *I acknowledged my sin to you,*
> *and I did not cover my iniquity;*
> *I said, "I will confess my transgressions to the Lord,"*
> *and you forgave the iniquity of my sin.* Selah

Insight 

During the dry season, the land of Israel is subject to strong sirocco winds blowing in from the desert. These winds create a hot, oppressive atmosphere. Perhaps this is what David had in mind when he spoke of the "heat of summer."

Day 2

5 In verses 3-4, David describes the torment he endured while living a lie before God ("when I kept silent . . . "). Complete these statements that describe how David suffered because of his sin:

"My bones ________________________________"
"[God's] hand ________________________________"
"My strength ________________________________"

! Key Point

Covering up sin is painful and destructive!

6 In your own words, how would you describe the consequences David experienced—physically, emotionally, and spiritually—as a result of his unwillingness to come clean with God?

For nearly a year David lived with God's convicting Spirit pressing down on his soul. Being silent about his wrongdoing—refusing to confess his sin—only deepened David's anguish. He deteriorated physically, emotionally, and spiritually.

If it can happen to David, it can happen to us. We are as vulnerable to sin's entrapment as he was and just as apt to try to conceal our failure. Refusing to be honest will reap the same rewards for us as it did for David. But here is the wonderful truth: *we have another choice!*

7 What did David finally do to return to the Lord and be freed from the weight of his guilt (Psalm 32:5)?

Day 2

8 How did God respond when David was finally willing to "uncover" his sin (v. 5)?

As we read the opening verses of Psalm 32, we can almost hear the joy and relief returning to David's spirit. When he finally let go of his pride, humbled himself, and got honest with God and others about his sin, heaven-sent relief poured over him. The weight of his iniquity was lifted, and his sin was carried away.

That can be your experience, too. As this passage indicates, God is willing to "cover" (with the blood of Christ) every sin that we are willing to "uncover" before Him. If David could experience the freedom and joy of a restored relationship with God after committing such great sin, you can know that "blessedness," too!

Simply begin with the matter at hand—whatever sin God may be convicting you of, whether "large" or "small." Remember, no sin is so large that God cannot forgive it; and no sin is so small that you can afford to keep it hidden.

Do you need to pause right now and be honest with God about some sin or failure in your life? How blessed is the person in whose spirit there is *no deceit!*

"Personal revival begins when the believer faces his sin honestly. Though painful, only honesty with God and others will enable the Christian to walk in purity and power."

—Jim Elliff

Day 2

Day 3: Truth Encounter

WALKING IN THE LIGHT

Having observed firsthand the life and ministry of Jesus, the apostle John marveled at the self-revealing nature of God. He wrote in his first epistle:

> *5This is the message we have heard from him and proclaim to you, that God is light, and in him is no darkness at all. 6If we say we have fellowship with him while we walk in darkness, we lie and do not practice the truth. 7But if we walk in the light, as he is in the light, we have fellowship with one another, and the blood of Jesus his Son cleanses us from all sin. 8If we say we have no sin, we deceive ourselves, and the truth is not in us. 9If we confess our sins, he is faithful and just to forgive us our sins and to cleanse us from all unrighteousness.* (1 John 1:5–9)

9 To what does John liken God (v. 5)? What does this metaphor tell us about God?

10 John says that because God is light, there is absolutely ________ ________ in Him (v. 5). What are the implications of this truth for our relationship with God?

! Key Point

Denying sin hinders fellowship with God.

11 What does John say about someone who claims to know God but persists in living a lifestyle that is contrary to God (v. 6)?

Day 3

12 Only when we "walk in the light" can we experience genuine fellowship with God and each other.What do you think it means to walk in the light?

13 What might cause a child of God to choose for a time to cover his or her sin, rather than walking in the light before God and others?

14 Who are we deceiving if we defend ourselves and claim to be innocent when we have in fact sinned (v. 8)? How does refusing to "walk in the light" affect our relationship with God and with others?

15 What must we do in order for our sins to be forgiven? On what basis is God "just" to forgive us our sins?

"If we feel we are innocent and have nothing to be broken about, it is not that these things are not there but that we have not seen them. We have been living in a realm of illusion about ourselves."

—Roy Hession

Insight

To "confess" our sin is to acknowledge our guilt before God—to agree with Him about our sin.

Day 3

John had known the joy of deep fellowship with God through Christ, and he wanted his readers to experience it, too. He reminds us that "God is light," and that when we cover up or refuse to acknowledge sin in our lives, we deceive ourselves and we cannot enjoy full fellowship with God or with each other. In fact, the person who habitually covers his sin has no basis for assurance that he is a child of God at all! Therefore, the willingness to be honest and confess our sin is an evidence of genuine salvation and is vital to experiencing God's forgiveness and restored fellowship when we sin as believers.

God wants to experience intimate fellowship with His children. That is possible only if we are honest with Him about the true condition of our heart as He knows it to be. No matter what you may have done, you can experience God's great love and amazing grace.

Day 4: Truth Encounter

BREAKING THE SILENCE

Silence is not golden when we use it to try to avoid the truth. Any attempt we make to hide from God—whether through silence or blatant lying—is absurd. Do we really believe God won't notice our sin or our efforts to conceal it? Apparently the disciples thought that was the case.

> [33]*[Jesus and the disciples] came to Capernaum. And when he was in the house he asked them, "What were you discussing on the way?"*
> [34]*But they kept silent, for on the way they had argued with one another about who was the greatest."* (Mark 9:33–34)

Key Point !

Our natural instinct is to avoid telling the truth about ourselves.

Isn't it amazing that a group of men so close to Christ would actually argue about which of them was most important? But they did, and Christ heard. He heard their argument, and He heard—through their silence—the sinful, proud attitudes that drove each of them to want to rule over the others.

In asking, "What were you discussing on the way?" Christ gave His disciples the opportunity to come clean, to "walk in the light" with Him. Instead they clammed up, hoping, no doubt, to avoid the truth. But a lie of omission is still a lie.

16 Why might Christ have waited to talk to the disciples rather than interrupting them while they were arguing? Why the delay in confronting them?

The disciples weren't the first to try to conceal their sin—Adam and Eve made the same futile attempt:

> [8]*And they heard the sound of the Lord God walking in the garden in the cool of the day, and the man and his wife hid themselves from the presence of the Lord God among the trees of the garden.* [9]*But the Lord God called to the man and said to him, "Where are you?"* (Genesis 3:8–9)

Day 4

After partaking of that which God had forbidden, Adam and Eve lost their innocence and discovered their guilt—and their nakedness. Immediately they went into concealment mode—sewing together fig leaves and looking for ways to blend into the landscape.

Have you ever thought how ridiculous it was for Adam and Eve to hope that a tree or a shrub would hide them from God? Have you ever thought how ridiculous it is for you and me to believe that by keeping silent about our sin we can throw God off the trail?

Just as interesting, however, is God's question: "Where are you?"(v. 9). Of course, God knew exactly where Adam and Eve were—He had seen the whole thing. He knew what they had done, and He knew where they were hiding.

17 Why do you think God asked Adam, "Where are you?" rather than simply telling him that He had seen everything he'd done?

18 What does this teach us about how God deals with us when we sin?

God faithfully gives His straying children opportunity to repent. He wants us to break the silence and admit our wrongdoing and/or sinful attitudes. He may do this by sending one of His servants to confront us (as Christ confronted the disciples), by causing us to suffer the consequences of our sin, or by allowing us to experience a deeper sense of His love and mercy. However God chooses to get our attention, the best response to Him is an honest one. Honesty is liberating.

Day4

The Scripture reminds us that we are accountable to an all-seeing, all-knowing God. We can be sure that every attempt to hide our sins will fail.

> *Nothing is covered up that will not be revealed, or hidden that will not be known.* (Luke 12:2)
>
> *And no creature is hidden from his sight, but all are naked and exposed to the eyes of him to whom we must give account.* (Hebrews 4:13)

19 In light of everything you have ever done, said, or thought, how do these verses make you feel? Do they reassure you, or do they make you uncomfortable?

In the verses leading up to Hebrews 4:13, we see that it is for our good and by God's mercy that He reveals the truth about us, no matter how shameful that truth may be. We learn that the reason God discloses our thoughts, actions, and motives is to bring to us peace (rest; Hebrews 4:11–12). God is not a bully; He is a Savior. He cannot be soft on sin. His justice requires holiness that we, in our humanity, do not have the capacity for. The demands of God's justice have been satisfied through the sacrificial, substitutionary death of Christ on the cross. However, we must come clean; we must confess. Silence only condemns by keeping us guilty.

Key Point !

Honesty about our sin opens the door for us to experience God's amazing grace.

Think about this . . . confessing our sin—breaking the silence—ushers in the forgiveness and cleansing of God. So, why hide? Why remain silent?

Is there something in your life that you know is displeasing to God, some attitude or past behavior? Are you trying to hide it from God, hoping He'll overlook it? Is God calling you to break the silence today?

Day 4

Day 5: Making It Personal

As a Christian seeking personal revival, you have an enemy in this ongoing struggle with deception. Jesus called him "a liar and the father of lies" (John 8:44). Dr. Bill Elliff observes:

> *[The devil] has successfully taught us that lying will produce some benefit.... We will be more respected, more appreciated, live more comfortably if we will just cover the truth. At all costs, we must never admit who we really are ("Think of how it would ruin our reputation!").*
>
> *The enemy is lying about lying! His very nature keeps him from telling the truth about the benefits of truthfulness. In reality, the wellspring of truthfulness yields a river of redemptive results. Honesty is as refreshing as a mountain stream and is God's intended means to wash and purify our hypocritical lives.*[2]

! Key Point

The longer we live a lie, the harder it is to come clean. The time to deal with it is now.

Yes, we have a strong enemy, but Christ's power is stronger still! Take time to meditate on the following Scriptures and to prayerfully respond to the questions below. As you do, allow the Holy Spirit to examine your heart. Ask God to show you any areas where you are not walking in the light with Him, with yourself, or with others. Thank Him for His grace and power to cleanse and revive honest hearts.

Honesty with God

Behold, You desire truth in the inward parts. (Psalm 51:6 NKJV)

- Do I often participate in corporate praise and prayer while my heart is cold, indifferent, or resistant to the Lord?
- Are my prayers honest? Do I say words that I think will impress God, or do I honestly communicate my real feelings and desires to Him?
- Do I honor Him with my lips when my mind and heart are far away? What am I really thinking about when I pray?
- When called upon to pray in public, am I more aware of God's presence or the fact that others are listening to what I say?
- Do I serve God out of a heart of genuine love and devotion, or do I have a subtle, secret desire to be noticed and applauded?
- Do I volunteer for service and good works to glorify God (Matthew 5:16) or to impress others?
- Am I quick to agree with God when His Spirit convicts me of sin, or do I tend to rationalize, justify, and defend myself?

- Do I see my sin as God sees it, or do I tend to think in terms of "weaknesses," "problems," "slip-ups,"or "personality quirks"?
- Do I love the truth so much that I actively and regularly ask God to search my heart and to reveal anything that is displeasing to Him?

Honesty with Myself

But be doers of the word, and not hearers only, deceiving yourselves. (James 1:22)

- Are there truths in God's Word that I know in my head or that I "preach" to others but am not practicing in my life?

If we say we have no sin, we deceive ourselves, and the truth is not in us. (1 John 1:8)

- Do I ignore, resist, or deny the conviction of God's Spirit or His Word in relation to my sin?

If anyone thinks he is something, when he is nothing, he deceives himself. (Galatians 6:3)

- Do I think more highly of myself than what God knows me to be? Do I have an inflated view of my gifts and my value to God and others?

> "Nothing can enter heaven which is not real; nothing erroneous, mistaken, conceited, hollow, professional, pretentious, insubstantial, can be smuggled through the gates. Only truth can dwell with the God of truth."
>
> —C. H. Spurgeon

Honesty with Others

Therefore, having put away falsehood, let each one of you speak the truth with his neighbor; for we are members one of another. (Ephesians 4:25)

- Do I sometimes seek to create a better impression of myself than is honestly true?
- Do I often leave others with the impression that I am more spiritually mature and committed than is actually true?
- Am I allowing my mate to believe that I am morally pure and faithful when I have failed morally?
- Am I covering up sins of my past rather than dealing with them biblically?
- Am I hiding specific sins or failures from my mate, a parent, a teacher, or an employer?
- Am I guilty of speaking graciously to others while harboring hatred or bitterness in my heart toward them?

"The only basis for real fellowship with God and man is to live out in the open with both."

—Roy Hession

- Do I put up walls to keep people from seeing the "real me"? Am I willing to let others into my life—to be honest about my spiritual needs, to ask for prayer about those needs, and to be accountable to others for areas where I need to grow or change?

---

[1] The Faith-Builder story in Lesson 3 is adapted from "The Great Pretender," *Spirit of Revival,* vol. 25, no. 2, September 1995, published by Life Action Ministries, pp. 7-9.

[2] Bill Elliff, "When I Kept Silent," *Spirit of Revival,* vol. 25, no. 2, September 1995, published by Life Action Ministries, p. 20.

Day 5

Seeking Him Together

Opening It Up

1. What part of this study or what Scripture has been most helpful to you thus far in understanding what revival means in your life? Why?

Talking It Over

2. The pastor in the Faith-Builder story admitted to having deceived others by what he *didn't* say. What are some other ways that we can be dishonest with people?

3. What are some of the areas of our lives that we most commonly try to hide from others?

4. Honesty works both ways. Why do you think other people might be afraid to be honest with us? What can we do to create greater freedom in the body of Christ to be honest with each other?

Seeking Him Together

5. Name some benefits of living a transparently honest life. Name some possible consequences of refusing to open our lives up to God and others.

6. Can you think of any Bible characters whose lives illustrate either the folly of pretense or the blessing of transparent honesty? Discuss your answers.

7. Read Psalm 32:1–5 aloud. Describe David's condition while he was living a lie.

Describe David's condition after he got honest and confessed.

What evidence do you see of complete, rather than partial, confession on David's part and forgiveness on God's part?

8. Read 1 John 1:5–9 aloud. How does "walking in the light" benefit us as individuals?

How does the body of Christ benefit when individual members "walk in the light"?

Tip 

"Honesty breeds honesty." When someone gets honest with brothers and sisters in Christ and is loved and supported, then others will also begin to lose their fear of being honest. Walking in the light restores and preserves unity in the church.

9. As you read through the "Making It Personal" questions on Day 5, was there any particular area of dishonesty with God, yourself, or others that the Lord pointed out to you?

Praying for Revival

To close, break into groups of two or three. Spend a few minutes "walking in the light" with each other. Provide an opportunity for each person to share at least one specific spiritual need in his/her life—perhaps an area of character that is not like Jesus, a particular sin struggled with, some relationship that needs to be resolved, etc.

Be as open and specific about your need as the Lord gives you freedom to be—of course, do not reflect negatively on anyone else or share details of sin that would be inappropriate to share with others.

After each person who wants to share has done so, take time to pray with and for each other about the needs that have been shared.

As the Lord prompts, pray for each other during the week and hold each other accountable in those areas.

Repentance: The Big Turnaround

We've learned that humility and honesty provide the fertile ground in which seeds of grace and revival can grow and bear fruit. The next step, then, is responding to God's conviction in genuine repentance. The concept of repentance is largely foreign to modern minds. Just what is repentance? What is its role in the life of a child of God? How do we know if we have truly repented? This study will explore these questions.

"Create in me a clean heart, O God, and renew a right spirit within me." **(Psalm 51:10)**

Psalm 51
Ezekiel 18:30–32
Luke 15:1–7
Acts 3:17–20

Day 1: **Faith-Builder Story**

1 What images, feelings, or reactions come to your mind when you think of "repentance"?

Read the story below of one woman's experience of repentance, and answer the questions that follow.

> After twenty-three years of being active in church life, I was burned out. I was tired of trying to live the Christian life, and in my heart I knew I was only giving lip service to the lordship of Christ. My heart had grown cold and calloused. I sought escape through sleep (having been addicted to over-the-counter sleeping pills for years), hobbies, novels, television—anything to fill the void and to avoid facing the barrenness of my life.
>
> Knowing that I was miserable and depressed, my husband tried to help. But I was convinced that he didn't care (Satan helped in perpetuating that lie!). I blamed him for my misery and the shallowness of my life. I thought that if he were different, then I would be different and our marriage and ministry would be different. I started living in a dream world, imagining what it would be like to be out of my marriage. I seriously entertained thoughts of divorce.
>
> Finally, I became so desperate that I just cried out for God to do a work in my life. And He heard! He answered my cries by showing me the truth about my heart and my life. He revealed my pride, which made me think that I deserved someone better. He showed me that my anger and bitterness toward my husband was really saying, "God, You made a mistake in the person You gave me for a husband."
>
> As God's Spirit worked in my heart, I slowly agreed with Him about my sins of pride and bitterness. God enabled me to stop blaming my husband and others for my condition. I literally came to life again. I began to turn away from the things I depended on instead of God. I laid my sleeping pills "on the altar," and God graciously delivered me from that bondage I had experienced for years. He delivered me from years of resentment toward my husband and gave me a new love for him. God truly revived my heart![1]

"I agreed with Him about my sins.... I literally came to life again."

2 What "keys" do you see in this woman's story that opened the door for her to experience personal revival?

3 Why do we often blame our circumstances or other people for our actions and our spiritual condition?

4 Read Psalm 51:1–6. Notice the complete absence of blame on David's part, once God convicted him of his wrongdoing. Why is it so important to accept full responsibility for our own sins?

5 Psalm 119:59 offers a good definition of repentance: *"When I think on my ways, I turn my feet to your testimonies."* How does this woman's story illustrate genuine repentance?

Day 2: Truth Encounter

THE CALL TO REPENTANCE

The role of repentance can be seen in every revival movement in history. One such revival happened in Romania in the 1970s. Christians there were once ridiculed as "Repenters" by their fellow countrymen, based on the emphasis given to repentance as being essential to conversion. There was a church in the town of Oradea, which had been languishing for a long time. Then God called a godly pastor to the area who was deeply committed to prayer. He began to preach on the theme "The Repenters Must Repent!"

! Key Point
Revival requires repentance.

God began to move in their hearts, and the Christians entered into a "covenant of repentance." They agreed to abstain from alcohol in any form and from lying to employers. (Both were common practices and were the issues in which God's conviction was most intense.) These Romanian believers became serious about forsaking the lifestyle that was common to the unbelievers around them.

The region was soon ablaze in revival and spiritual awakening. Many became believers and were baptized. A Bible college was established and became the largest producer of national church leaders in Eastern Europe. Several years later, when the Communist regime collapsed, those who were forming the new government sought the counsel of the church leaders in Oradea. The influence of the "Repenters" was felt throughout that portion of the world.

! Key Point
Repentance involves returning to the Lord, forsaking sin, and obeying God.

Like our Romanian brothers and sisters, every child of God who is seeking after Him with a whole heart must realize that repentance is not an option but a requirement. God says, "Return to Me, and I will return to you" (Malachi 3:7). The act of returning to the Lord—forsaking known sin and obeying what He says—is repentance. This is a crucial step for all who are seeking God for revival.

Calls to repent abound throughout the Bible. In the Old Testament, the nations of Israel and Judah repeatedly strayed from the Lord, and each time God sent messengers to plead with His people to return to Him.

This same message is a prominent theme throughout the New Testament as well—from beginning to end.

6 Read Matthew 3:2 and 4:17. What was the message preached by John the Baptist and the Lord Jesus?

7 Read Revelation 2:5, 16, 21–22; 3:3, 19. In the final book of the Bible, what is the recurring exhortation Jesus gives to the churches?

8 How often do you think a person must repent to be in a right relationship with God?

- ❍ Only once, when the person believes in Christ for salvation.
- ❍ During special church services when others are also "rededicating" their lives to God.
- ❍ Daily, in order to keep a clean slate before God.
- ❍ At salvation and anytime thereafter that God convicts the person of sin.

Key Point !

Repentance is for Christians as well as non-Christians.

An attitude of repentance is crucial in our initial coming to Christ for salvation. The New Testament apostles called both Jews and Greeks to respond in "repentance toward God and faith in our Lord Jesus Christ" (Acts 20:21). To become a Christian, a person must repent—*turn away from*—an old way of life and *turn to* Christ for forgiveness and salvation.

Yet repentance does not end there. This same attitude is also needed in our ongoing relationship with God. Christians will still be tempted to sin even though they have been given a new nature. They will sometimes yield to temptation and choose to sin. However, the inclination of those in God's family will be to humbly confess and forsake sin whenever they are confronted with it in their lives.

Day 2

At one point in his ministry, the apostle Paul was forced to send a strong disciplinary letter to the church in Corinth, to address a particular issue that needed to be corrected. In the book of 2 Corinthians, he commends the Christians there for responding to his earlier rebuke with godly sorrow and true repentance.

> [9]*I rejoice, not because you were grieved, but because you were grieved into repenting. For you felt a godly grief, so that you suffered no loss through us.*
>
> [10]*For godly grief produces a repentance that leads to salvation without regret, whereas worldly grief produces death.* [11]*For see what earnestness this godly grief has produced in you, but also what eagerness to clear yourselves, what indignation, what fear, what longing, what zeal, what punishment! At every point you have proved yourselves innocent in the matter.* (2 Corinthians 7:9–11)

"The believer in Christ is a 'lifelong' repenter. He begins with repentance, and ends with repentance."

—Jim Elliff

9 The Corinthian believers did more than just *claim* to have repented. What was the evidence that they were truly repentant in this matter?

10 Based on this passage, how would you describe the difference between being *remorseful* over sin ("worldly grief") and being *repentant* ("godly grief")?

From the point of regeneration until the day we are finally free from the presence of sin, our heart attitude must *always* be: "Lord, I am willing to forsake any sin that You show me, in order to have a pure heart and glorify You."

In other words, once a repenter, always a repenter.

Day 3: Truth Encounter

A CHANGE OF MIND

Before sin becomes an act, it is first a thought. We call that *being tempted.* If we do not call out to God for help and deliverance in these moments of temptation, or if we allow ourselves to indulge the thought of sin in our minds, we will likely commit the sin eventually.

Once we sin, God gives us a means to escape from sin's lure and grip, through the power of the Holy Spirit who lives within us. We call this *conviction*—that internal "call" to turn around and change direction when we have sinned.

Just as sin begins in our minds (as a temptation), so repentance begins in our minds as the Holy Spirit brings conviction. The mind is a crucial part of our spiritual anatomy, as the following verses show:

> *[Jesus] said to him, "You shall love the Lord your God with all your heart, and with all your soul, and with all your mind."* (Matthew 22:37)

> [1]*I appeal to you therefore, brothers, by the mercies of God, to present your bodies as a living sacrifice, holy and acceptable to God, which is your spiritual worship.* [2]*Do not be conformed to this world, but be transformed by the renewal of your mind, that by testing you may discern what is the will of God, what is good and acceptable and perfect.* (Romans 12:1–2)

11 What role do our minds play in our pleasing God and being transformed into the likeness of Christ?

Since we first respond to spiritual matters with our minds, "renewing the mind" must include training it to

- recognize and run from temptation, and
- respond quickly to the Holy Spirit's conviction.

Insight 

The Greek word *metanoeo,* translated as *repentance* in the New Testament, means "to think differently about something or to have a change of mind."

Key Point 

Repentance begins in the mind as conviction of sin.

Day 3

12 How can we train our minds to resist temptation and to respond to the Spirit's conviction?

"Repentance is to
leave
The sin we loved
before,
And show that
we in earnest
grieve
By doing so
no more."

—C. H. Spurgeon

Once the Spirit convicts us of sin, how do we know if we have truly repented? Read the following passages for the answer.

John the Baptist warned people to:

> *Bear fruit in keeping with repentance.* (Matthew 3:8)

In the book of Revelation, Jesus said to the church in Ephesus:

> [4] *I have this against you, that you have abandoned the love you had at first.* [5] *Remember therefore from where you have fallen;* ***repent, and do the works you did at first.*** *If not, I will come to you and remove your lampstand from its place, unless you repent.* (2:4–5, emphasis added)

13 According to these verses, what is the evidence that you have truly repented?

❍ Feeling bad about my sin.

❍ Confessing my sin and saying, "I'm sorry."

❍ A change in my behavior.

! Key Point

Real repentance influences behavior.

Repentance cannot be considered genuine unless there is outward evidence—*a change of behavior.* It's not just a matter of feeling bad about our sin. If repentance is real, it will show itself. The outward manifestation of repentance may be instantaneous or it may be seen over time. The length of time for real change may depend on the nature of the sin and how long one has been involved in it, or other variables. But sooner or later, there will be a change in behavior.

14 From what you've studied thus far, write out a brief description of what repentance "looks like" in the life of a believer. (You may want to memorize the simple definition suggested here.)

Definition 

Repentance is a change of mind that results in a change of behavior.

15 Briefly describe a time in your life, *since becoming a Christian,* when you had "left your first love" or God convicted you of a particular sin, and you truly repented. What was wrong about your thinking or the direction you were headed? How did your thinking and your behavior change as an evidence of your repentance?

Day 3

Day 4: Truth Encounter

RESPONDING TO GOD'S CALL

! Key Point

When God calls us to repent, it's time to act.

God's call to repentance may not be an easy or pleasant experience. Sometimes He uses our own conscience to convict us. Other times He may allow us to "get caught." He may even send one of His servants to rebuke us. No matter how God deals with our sin, it is important that we understand three things:

1. *The very fact that God reveals sin in our lives and urges us to repent is evidence of His great love, mercy, and kindness.* Even in the life of a Christian, sin leads to destruction. Something in our lives will break down as a result of unconfessed sin. God does not want this for His children, and He will "wound" us temporarily, if necessary, in order to restore us. He will not leave us on a path of destruction without giving us an opportunity to repent. (See Romans 2:1–10.)

2. *The best time for us to respond to God is at the moment of conviction.* The longer we delay, the harder we resist His Spirit, the more difficult it becomes to humble ourselves and repent.

3. *God never asks anything of us that He does not provide the grace to do.* In terms of repenting, this means that no matter how strong the bondage of sin or how long we have been involved in it, God can deliver us by His grace. (See 1 Corinthians 10:13 and 2 Corinthians 12:9.)

"The more we realize our indebtedness to God's grace, and the more we see of the sufferings of Christ in order to effect our redemption, the more do we hate sin, and the more do we lament that we ever fell into it."

—C. H. Spurgeon

In order to maintain a lifestyle of repentance, we must keep our hearts in a posture of humility. Proud hearts do not respond well to God—a truth illustrated in the life of King Uzziah. Read the passage below and then answer the questions that follow.

> [3]*Uzziah was sixteen years old when he began to reign, and he reigned fifty-two years in Jerusalem. His mother's name was Jecoliah of Jerusalem. [4]And he did what was right in the eyes of the Lord, according to all that his father Amaziah had done. [5]He set himself to seek God in the days of Zechariah, who instructed him in the fear of God, and as long as he sought the Lord, God made him prosper. . . .*
>
> [16]*But when he was strong, he grew proud, to his destruction. For he was unfaithful to the Lord his God and entered the temple of the Lord to burn incense on the altar of incense.*
>
> [17]*But Azariah the priest went in after him, with eighty priests of the Lord who were men of valor, [18]and they withstood King Uzziah and said to him, "It is not for you, Uzziah, to burn incense to the Lord, but for the*

priests the sons of Aaron, who are consecrated to burn incense. Go out of the sanctuary, for you have done wrong, and it will bring you no honor from the Lord God."

19Then Uzziah was angry. Now he had a censer in his hand to burn incense, and when he became angry with the priests, leprosy broke out on his forehead in the presence of the priests in the house of the Lord, by the altar of incense.
20And Azariah the chief priest and all the priests looked at him, and behold, he was leprous in his forehead! And they rushed him out quickly, and he himself hurried to go out, because the Lord had struck him.

21And King Uzziah was a leper to the day of his death, and being a leper lived in a separate house, for he was excluded from the house of the Lord. (2 Chronicles 26:3–5, 16–21)

16 God prospered Uzziah because he sought after the Lord. What changed to cause Uzziah to act unfaithfully to God?

17 While in the very act of sin, Uzziah was given an opportunity to repent. How did God call Uzziah to repentance?

18 How did Uzziah respond when confronted with the truth? What were the consequences?

Day 4

Repentance turns our hearts aright, as one would turn a capsized boat over to an upright position. The purpose of repentance is not to make us feel better about ourselves but to restore us to a right relationship with God, so that our lives may again bring glory to Him and be used for His purposes. That's what personal revival is all about!

! Key Point

Repentance enables us to glorify God.

So what does a repenter look like? Consider the following statements that describe some ways that a person who is sensitive to God's work of conviction will respond.

- *A repenter renews his mind with truth from Scripture consistently.* He is aware that the battle against temptation is first waged in the mind and that the process of repentance begins there as well.
- *A repenter responds to God immediately.* At the first sign of conviction, he agrees with God about his sin, turns away from it, and turns toward the Lord.
- *A repenter obeys God completely.* His repentance is thorough, and he does not cast a longing look back at sin. He forsakes the temporary pleasure of sin for the abiding joy of God's blessing.
- *A repenter follows God personally.* He does not base his commitment to God on what others are doing. "Though no one joins me, still I will follow" expresses the attitude of his heart.
- *A repenter accepts God's discipline faithfully.* Realizing that sin has consequences, he accepts the Lord's discipline as an act of love and as a reminder when he next faces temptation.

"Repentance is hating what you once loved, and loving what you once hated."

—Jim Elliff

19 Note the verbs used in the description above. What is our part in repentance? What is God's part?

20 Based on this description, could you call yourself a true "repenter"? Why or why not? Write a brief prayer asking God to grant you a repentant heart.

Day 5: **Making It Personal**

You've discovered what repentance is. Now it's time to look at your own heart. Prayerfully and honestly answer the following questions. As you do, ask God to reveal areas where you may be resisting His loving conviction. You may want to record a personal response to specific questions, as the Lord shines His light on your heart.

1. Have I ever experienced the repentance that characterizes genuine salvation?
2. Does sin in my life bother me?
3. Do I have an attitude that says, "Lord, everything I know to be sin, and everything You show me in the future to be sin, I am willing to forsake"?
4. Am I willing to call my wrong actions "sin," rather than viewing them as weaknesses, "struggles," or personality traits?
5. Am I more concerned about grieving God than about the consequences of my sin?
6. Am I willing to accept personal responsibility for my actions, without pointing the finger of blame at anyone else?
7. Am I willing to take whatever steps may be necessary to make complete restitution for my sin?
8. Have I, at any time in the past year, experienced genuine repentance, resulting in a change of attitude and/or behavior?
9. Has God convicted me of any specific sins in my life that I have never truly repented of? If so, am I willing to repent of those sins here and now?
10. Am I willing to be accountable to another believer in those areas of my life where I have experienced past failure, so that I may develop new patterns of victory?

Is God calling you to turn away from any particular sin in your life? Responding to God is more important than whatever you were planning on doing next. If God is speaking, the time to respond is *now.* Will you humble yourself and allow Him to begin restoring you? Remember, He loves you, offers grace to cover any sin, and longs for you to walk in freedom and joy.

> "There must be a divorce between you and your sins. Not a mere separation for a season, but a clear divorce."
>
> —C. H. Spurgeon

> "True repentance is to cease from sin."
>
> —St. Ambrose

Write a prayer expressing your response to what God has shown you about your heart and any need you may have for repentance. (The conviction of the Holy Spirit typically deals with specific issues in our lives, so be as specific as possible in your response, rather than just dealing with generalities.)

[1] The Faith-Builder story in Lesson 4 is adapted from "Rescued from Pretense," *Spirit of Revival*, vol. 19, no. 1, July 1989, p. 22, published by Life Action Ministries.

Day5

Seeking Him Together

Opening It Up

1. What is repentance, and why is it so crucial in the process of both personal and corporate revival?

Talking It Over

2. The woman in the Faith-Builder story blamed her husband and others for her problems. How does our tendency to blame others hinder the work of God in our lives?

3. What evidences of repentance did you see in this woman's life?

4. Review the story of the Romanian revival in Day 2. How does this account show the importance of both individual and corporate repentance?

Tip +

A key means to continued growth in humility and repentance is accountability combined with mutual encouragement.

Seeking Him **Together**

5. What might it look like in our day if believers were to begin to live as "repenters"? How would our churches change? How might the impact be seen in our culture?

6. How does repentance affect both our mind and our behavior?

7. When God brings conviction of sin to the heart of one of His children, what does it tell us about Him?

8. When is the best time to respond to God's conviction and His call to repentance? Why?

9. Share one area of your life where you have experienced true repentance *since* becoming a Christian.

10. If you're willing to volunteer, share with the group how God is dealing with you (or has recently dealt with you) regarding some specific need for repentance.

Tip 

If God is dealing with you on a very personal sin issue or one that involves other people, use discretion in any sharing you might do.

Praying for Revival

If time allows, close your time with a responsive reading based on Psalm 51, King David's prayer of repentance. (For the story of David's sin, see 2 Samuel 11:1–12:15.) Make this your prayer now and throughout the coming week.

LEADER: *Have mercy on me, O God, according to your steadfast love; according to your abundant mercy blot out my transgressions.*

GROUP: We depend on You alone for mercy and compassion. We have no other source of forgiveness.

LEADER: *Wash me thoroughly from my iniquity, and cleanse me from my sin!*

GROUP: We need You to cleanse us completely from every act of sin and from our desire to sin.

LEADER: *For I know my transgressions, and my sin is ever before me.*

GROUP: Guilt is our constant companion when we refuse to repent.

LEADER: *Against You, You only, have I sinned and done what is evil in Your sight, so that You may be justified in Your words and blameless in Your judgment.*

"Repentance is not a mere feeling of sorrow or contrition for an act of wrongdoing. The regret I feel when I act impatiently or speak crossly is not repentance. . . . Repentance is contrition for what we are in our fundamental beings, that we are wrong in our deepest roots because our internal government is by Self and not by God."

—Florence Allshorn

Seeking Him **Together**

GROUP: All our sin is committed against You and while You are watching. You are just. You have every right to deal with our sin.

LEADER: *Behold, I was brought forth in iniquity, and in sin did my mother conceive me.*

GROUP: Our human nature is bent toward sin and has been from birth.

LEADER: *Behold, You delight in truth in the inward being, and You teach me wisdom in the secret heart.*

GROUP: You know us through and through, and You want us to be completely honest with You about the true condition of our hearts.

LEADER: *Purge me with hyssop, and I shall be clean; wash me, and I shall be whiter than snow. Let me hear joy and gladness; let the bones that you have broken rejoice. Hide your face from my sins, and blot out all my iniquities. Create in me a clean heart, O God, and renew a right spirit within me. Cast me not away from your presence, and take not your Holy Spirit from me.*

GROUP: You must cleanse us; we cannot cleanse ourselves or promise to do better. Only You can give us a clean heart and a renewed spirit.

LEADER: *Restore to me the joy of your salvation, and uphold me with a willing spirit. Then I will teach transgressors your ways, and sinners will return to you.*

GROUP: Only You can grant the joy that is the fruit of true repentance. By the power of Your Holy Spirit, You can restore us, protect us from sin, and use us as instruments of grace in the lives of others.

LEADER: *Deliver me from bloodguiltiness, O God, O God of my salvation, and my tongue will sing aloud of your righteousness. O Lord, open my lips, and my mouth will declare your praise. For you will not delight in sacrifice, or I would give it; you will not be pleased with a burnt offering. The sacrifices of God are a broken spirit; a broken and contrite heart, O God, you will not despise.*

GROUP: The only worship and service a sinful heart can offer You is to confess and repent.

LEADER: *Do good to Zion in your good pleasure; build up the walls of Jerusalem; then you will delight in right sacrifices, in burnt offerings and whole burnt offerings; then bulls will be offered on your altar.*

GROUP: Restore us to worship and help us serve You again!

Lesson 5

Grace:

God's Provision for Every Need

Thus far in our study, we have seen the need for humility, honesty, and repentance as we seek the Lord. In the following lessons, we will consider several additional keys to experiencing true revival: personal holiness, complete obedience, a clear conscience toward God and others, forgiveness, and sexual purity. At this stage in the process, it could be easy to feel overwhelmed with a sense of conviction, failure, and guilt; some may even be tempted to give up on seeking God for revival.

The good news is that God does not ask us to meet His requirements on our own—in fact, He knows we *can't* live humble, holy, obedient lives without Him. God makes available to every one of His children an incredible resource to make it possible for us to live a godly life. That amazing, extravagant provision is called . . . *grace.*

"Let us then with confidence draw near to the throne of grace, that we may receive mercy and find grace to help in time of need." **(Hebrews 4:16)**

John 1:14–18
Romans 5:12–17
Titus 2:11–14

Day 1: **Faith-Builder Story**

1 Through the course of this study, you may have struggled with a particular change God has been prompting you to make or a sin you know He wants you to confess and forsake. Check any of the following feelings you have had in response:

❍ "I really want to obey God, but I can't—it's just too hard."

❍ "I'm afraid to do what I know I need to do."

❍ "I know what God wants me to do, but honestly, I just don't have the desire to do it."

❍ "I feel overwhelmed by my guilt and failure before God."

❍ "I'll never be able to measure up to what I should be."

❍ "I've got to work harder to get my act together so I can be more godly."

If you have had any of these thoughts—be encouraged! In this week's study, you will learn how God's grace can meet each of these needs and how you can experience more of His abundant grace in your life.

Read the following story about sin and grace, and answer the questions that follow.

"Laurie didn't think I could be hiding any sins of great magnitude, but reality was much different."

> On the surface, things looked good. We were active in our church. The oldest of our three children was a Christian with a deep desire to serve the Lord. I was a respected professor at a nearby state university. But beneath the surface things were not so calm. One child had become rebellious, and my love for my wife, Laurie, had grown cold. I hadn't worn my wedding ring for years.
>
> When our church hosted a revival crusade, God dealt with my wife and me in very personal ways. We learned that we could not live the Christian life apart from God's grace, and that the only way to experience that grace in our lives was to humble ourselves. This was no time to be half-hearted. God was extending an opportunity to "come clean" and be revived. Laurie didn't think I could be hiding any sins of great magnitude, but the reality was much different. I knew the costs would be high as I began admitting the truth to her.
>
> One "secret sin" I had kept hidden for many years was that I had stolen money from a company through "skimming"—invoicing a smaller sale

than what I had actually charged the customer, then pocketing the difference. Also, I had cheated on a field exam while acquiring my Ph.D. Even though I had studied faithfully, I panicked the night before the exam. As a teaching assistant I had keys to where the exams were stored, so I copied the exam questions. Out of guilt, I had never been able to hang my diploma on my office wall.

I had thought many times about owning up to the stealing and the cheating. The worst that could happen was losing my degree and my job. These were no small consequences, but they paled in comparison to what I thought would happen if I admitted to Laurie yet one more hidden sin: I had been unfaithful to her several times.

As I confessed these things to Laurie, she was taken by complete surprise. She had known for a long time that our marriage wasn't in good shape, but we respected each other and both loved our kids. Now everything she had believed about me was shattered. But somehow, by the grace of God, and with the counsel and support of Christian friends, Laurie met my confessions with forgiveness. Furthermore, she committed to help me make the necessary restitution for the wrongs I had done, while working together to rebuild our marriage. Truly we were on a journey of grace.

"We drove for ten hours across four states. I met first with my former boss, confessed the thefts, and asked for his forgiveness."

We drove for ten hours across four states. I met first with my former boss, confessed the thefts, and asked for his forgiveness. He expressed considerable surprise that I had done such a thing, yet readily gave his forgiveness.

"Truly we were on a journey of grace."

Next we met with my doctoral adviser. With many tears, I confessed the cheating and handed him my diploma. Again, God's grace had already been working, evidenced by his compassionate response. He explained that he saw no reason to revoke my diploma since seeing the exam questions only hours before taking the test could not have made any appreciable difference in my performance. I was humbled by his forgiveness. He informed us that he too was a Christian and encouraged me to continue to follow through with what God was doing in my life.

In just twenty-four hours God had worked miracle after miracle on our behalf. With each step of humility and obedience, God had begun to pour His incredible grace into our lives. Laurie and I had discovered a love for each other that neither of us had thought possible given our past—the kind of love that comes only from doing things God's way. Our hearts overflowed with joy as we talked about what God had done and what He was going to do.

2 What risks did this man face in confessing his sin to his wife, his former boss, and his doctoral supervisor?

3 What consequences did he risk if he chose to keep these things hidden?

4 What enabled him to come clean?

5 David was a man who was desperately aware of his need for God's grace and wasn't afraid to ask for it! Underline each phrase in this passage that refers to asking God for help. Circle each phrase that indicates how God responds when His children call upon Him.

! Key Point

God will provide all the grace we need to face any demand.

1 Incline your ear, O Lord, and answer me,
for I am poor and needy.
2 Preserve my life, for I am godly;
save your servant, who trusts in you—you are my God.
3 Be gracious to me, O Lord,
for to you do I cry all the day.
4 Gladden the soul of your servant,
for to you, O Lord, do I lift up my soul.
5 For you, O Lord, are good and forgiving,
abounding in steadfast love to all who call upon you.

Day 1

[6] *Give ear, O Lord, to my prayer;*
listen to my plea for grace.
[7] *In the day of my trouble I call upon you,*
for you answer me. (Psalm 86:1–7)

6 How does calling upon God express humility? What assurance does this psalm give you that God's grace is available to meet any needs you expressed in question 1?

Day 2: **Truth Encounter**

SAVING GRACE

If a young man is killed through some random act of violence, and his father tracks down the guilty person and kills him, we would call that *vengeance.* If, however, the father calls the police and the murderer is arrested, tried, convicted, and executed, we'd call that *justice.* If, at the trial, the father pleads for the guilty man's life to be spared and the judge and jury consent, we'd call that *mercy.*

Now imagine this: in addition to pleading for the guilty one to be spared, the father actually appeals to the judge to release the offender into his custody and care. Miraculously gaining approval, the father takes the young man into his heart and home, adopts him, and raises him and loves him as his own son . . . that would be *grace!*

No word brings greater joy to the heart of a follower of Christ than *grace.* Grace is the free gift of God to those who have sinned against Him and deserve only His wrath. Grace is that which God gives us to meet His requirements and to face the difficulties of life. The most magnificent display of God's grace is seen in our salvation, as described for us in Ephesians 2:1–9:

> *[1]And you were dead in the trespasses and sins in which you once walked,. . . [3]and were by nature children of wrath, like the rest of mankind.*
>
> *[4]But God, being rich in mercy, because of the great love with which he loved us, even when we were dead in our trespasses, made us alive together with Christ,. . . [7]so that in the coming ages he might show the immeasurable riches of his grace in kindness toward us in Christ Jesus.*
>
> *[8]For by grace you have been saved through faith. And this is not your own doing; it is the gift of God, [9]not a result of works, so that no one may boast.*

! Key Point

By His grace, God pardons guilty sinners and reconciles them to Himself.

7 Make a list of the words or phrases in these verses that describe what our condition was like apart from the grace of God.

Our situation was truly desperate. We had no hope…no possibility of overcoming sin's dominion on our own. No power to initiate our own salvation. No potential of ever having a right relationship with God. We could not do *anything* to change or improve our situation. If our sinful condition had made us only sick or weak, we might have entertained hopes of getting better. But we weren't sick; we were dead. Someone had to infuse life into us. Someone did.

8 In our fallen, sinful condition, God would have been just to let us suffer the consequences of His wrath for all eternity. Instead, He poured out on us just the opposite. List four qualities found in Ephesians 2:1-9 that God bestowed on us when we were "dead in our trespasses":

M __________
L __________
G __________
K __________

9 According to these verses, what was the outcome of God's gracious gift and His intervention on our behalf?

____

"Dark is the stain that
we cannot hide;
What can avail
to wash it away?
Look! there is flowing
a crimson tide—
Whiter than snow
you may be today.
Marvelous, infinite,
matchless grace,
Freely bestowed on
all who believe!
You that are longing
to see His face,
Will you this moment
His grace receive?"

—Julia H. Johnston

Humankind's sinful condition was more than an annoyance to God. Sin was not something we could apologize for, thereby patching up the relationship as if we'd simply had a disagreement with God. We were children of wrath—guilty and condemned. Not a pleasant thought, is it—that our eternal soul sat on death row? *But where there is God there is grace, and where there is grace there is pardon.*

By His grace God did for us what we could not do for ourselves: He gave us life for death and pardon for condemnation. At the cross, God satisfied His own vengeance, met His own demands of justice, extended mercy, and then added the surprise of His grace. Having punished sin, God forgave sinners; then He went on to adopt all who would believe, making them fellow heirs with His only Son. Such is the extravagant love and grace of God.

10 What phrases in the passage we have been considering make clear that we could not earn or deserve God's grace?

"The love of God is manifested brilliantly in His grace toward undeserving sinners. And that is exactly what grace is: God's love flowing *freely* to the *unlovely.*"

—A. W. Tozer

God's grace is never given as a reward for anything we could possibly do to merit it. As we explore further the riches of God's grace, not only in salvation but also in our sanctification, we must remember that God's grace is always a *gift* given to the undeserving. That's what makes it so amazing.

Have you received the gift of salvation that God offers to you through His grace? If not, will you now? Call a pastor or a friend who belongs to Christ and ask him to pray with you.

If you have received God's saving grace, have you come to take it for granted or lost a sense of the wonder of what God has done for you? Take a few minutes to pray, thanking God for giving you life and saving your soul. You may want to sing a hymn or chorus such as "Amazing Grace."

Day 2

Day 3: Truth Encounter

SANCTIFYING GRACE

Once we receive God's saving grace, we don't automatically become spiritual giants who have arrived and have it all together. As redeemed children of God, we continue to be helpless and needy apart from Him. We need God's grace—every moment of every day—to sanctify us and to conform us to the image of Christ.

Key Point !

We are utterly dependent on God's grace to live the Christian life.

11 Check any of the following statements that are sometimes true of you.

There are times when . . .

❍ I am strongly tempted to sin.

❍ I give in to temptation and choose to sin.

❍ I feel overpowered by the pull of a particular sin in my life.

❍ I know what God wants me to do, but just don't have the desire to obey Him.

❍ I really want to obey God, but I don't seem to have the power to do so.

❍ I feel totally inadequate to do some task I know God has called me to do.

If you've been a Christian for longer than a few weeks, you have probably experienced all of the above! Such feelings cause many Christians to become discouraged, to despair, or even to want to give up: *I'm such a failure . . . this Christian life is just too hard!*

"Grace is a dynamic force that does more than affect our standing with God by crediting us with righteousness. Grace affects our experience as well. . . . Grace is a way of life."

—Larry Richards

The fact is, even as Christians we do fail, we are weak, and we do have needs. How do we deal with these challenges? Thankfully, through Jesus Christ, God has provided just what we need to deal with each of these situations. This wonderful, supernatural provision is the same gift that made it possible for us to be saved. It is God's amazing *grace.*

As Christians, we recognize that we are *saved* by God's grace alone, totally apart from our own effort or ability. However, many Christians mistakenly think that once they're saved, it's up to them to live the Christian life—that they can somehow be *sanctified* by their own effort or ability. So they struggle and strive to be "good Christians," failing to realize that they cannot live the Christian life apart from God's grace, any more than they could be saved apart from God's grace. In this session and the next, we will consider some of the specific ways we need God's grace as believers.

12 What do the following Scriptures tell us about God's provision when we are tempted to sin?

> *No temptation has overtaken you that is not common to man. God is faithful, and he will not let you be tempted beyond your ability, but with the temptation he will also provide the way of escape, that you may be able to endure it.* (1 Corinthians 10:13)

> "Grace is not simply leniency when we have sinned. Grace is the enabling gift of God not to sin. Grace is power, not just pardon."
>
> —John Piper

> [15]*For we do not have a high priest who is unable to sympathize with our weaknesses, but one who in every respect has been tempted as we are, yet without sin.* [16]*Let us then with confidence draw near to the throne of grace, that we may receive mercy and find grace to help in time of need.* (Hebrews 4:15–16)

> *For sin will have no dominion over you, since you are not under law but under grace.* (Romans 6:14)

What about when we fail and give in to temptation? It is God's grace that convicts us when we sin and gives us the ability and desire to confess and forsake our sin. Have you ever sinned so greatly or so frequently that you felt overwhelmed by guilt and condemnation? You couldn't imagine how God could possibly forgive you—*again!* Once again, God's grace is what you need.

13 According to the Bible, we are told that "where sin abounded, grace abounded much more" (Romans 5:20 NKJV). Paraphrase that verse in your own words. How does this truth practically apply to our lives as believers?

If God extends grace and forgiveness to us when we confess and repent of our sin, does that mean we are free to sin whenever and however we want to, as long as we intend to confess it? That might sound ludicrous, but some first-century believers actually suggested that if one's sin served to put a spotlight on the grace of God, perhaps we should just feel free to sin all the more! The apostle Paul addressed that line of thinking in no uncertain terms:

> [1]*What shall we say then? Are we to continue in sin that grace may abound?* [2]*By no means! How can we who died to sin still live in it?* (Romans 6:1–2)

> [11]*For the grace of God has appeared, bringing salvation for all people,* [12]*training us to renounce ungodliness and worldly passions, and to live self-controlled, upright, and godly lives in the present age.* (Titus 2:11–12)

14 According to these verses, how should God's grace be a restraint, rather than a license to sin?

Not only do we need God's grace when we are tempted and when we sin; we need His grace to do *anything* that is pleasing to Him. In fact, there is not one single aspect of the Christian life that we can handle *apart* from God's grace!

The apostle Paul reminded the Philippian believers that "it is God who works in you both to *will* and to *do* for His good pleasure" (Philippians 2:13, NKJV). God's grace is the dynamic quality of His life within us that gives us both the *desire* and the *power* to obey God.

God is fully aware that we are incapable of godly living in spite of our best intentions or efforts. His grace is His supernatural supply for all that we lack. He promises to equip and empower us to do whatever He requires of us.

Insight

In 2 Corinthians 8–9, Paul exhorts the believers in relation to the grace of giving. As with everything else God asks us to do, it is His grace that enables us to "abound in every good work."

> *And God is able to make all grace abound to you, so that having all sufficiency in all things at all times, you may abound in every good work.* (2 Corinthians 9:8)

15 Circle the words *all* and *abound* each time they appear in this verse. How does this verse encourage you as you consider the various tasks and responsibilities God has entrusted to you?

Day 4: Truth Encounter

SUFFERING GRACE

Thus far in this lesson we have considered the grace of God that secures our salvation; we have also seen that it is God's grace that sanctifies us. Now we turn to look at the grace God provides when we are called to suffer.

As Elisabeth Elliot has said, suffering is "having what you don't want, or wanting what you don't have"; it can range in scope and severity from "traffic jams to taxes to tumors."

You (or someone you love) may be facing a situation or a season that seems beyond your limits of sanity and strength. You may be dealing with illness, grief, a family crisis, or financial pressure. You feel pressed against a wall, with no hope of relief or help in sight. Whatever the circumstances, you can be sure that you (or your loved one) are in the crosshairs of grace. God's grace is available and sufficient for your need—He will provide a way for you to endure.

Key Point !

God's grace enables us to endure the deepest pain.

The apostle Paul knew what it was to endure relentless hardship and pain. For the sake of Christ, he suffered rejection and persecution that would have caused many to give up.

Insight 

Scripture does not tell us what Paul's "thorn in the flesh" was.The Greek word translated *thorn* means a "tent stake" and was used to speak of a wooden stake used for impaling someone. Whatever it was, Paul's "thorn" was not merely a "splinter" or a "sliver." It was a major affliction—chronic or recurring, and excruciatingly painful.

At some point, Paul was afflicted with a "thorn in the flesh"—some sort of malady that caused him to suffer greatly. Repeatedly, Paul implored the Lord to relieve him of the problem. As we see in 2 Corinthians 12, the Lord did not choose to grant that desire. Instead, the Lord gave Paul exactly what he needed to deal with the thorn and to turn it into a blessing:

> [8] *Three times I pleaded with the Lord about this, that it should leave me.* [9] *But he said to me, "My grace is sufficient for you, for my power is made perfect in weakness." Therefore I will boast all the more gladly of my weaknesses, so that the power of Christ may rest upon me.* (vv. 8–9)

16 What does this passage reveal about the grace of God?

Day 4

> "When God declared to Paul, . . . 'My grace is sufficient for you,' He affirmed the total sufficiency of His grace for every need in life. . . . God's grace was sufficient for the deepest pain Paul (or any other believer) could ever experience."
>
> —John MacArthur

17 How do our weaknesses and needs provide a showcase for God's power?

18 How did Paul respond to the assurance of God's grace?

> "When you are in the furnace, your Father keeps His eye on the clock and His hand on the thermostat."
>
> —Warren Wiersbe

The apostle Peter wrote his epistles to strengthen and encourage believers who were going through intense suffering. The grace of God is a prominent theme in his letters. At the end of 1 Peter, he reminds his readers that the "God of all grace" is actively, directly, and personally involved in the lives of His children, even when they are suffering and may feel He has forgotten them:

> *After you have suffered a little while, the God of all grace, who has called you to his eternal glory in Christ, will himself restore, confirm, strengthen, and establish you.* (1 Peter 5:10)

19 When we are in the midst of a "crisis" or experiencing chronic pain or hardship, we sometimes feel as if "this will go on forever!" What perspective does 1 Peter 5:10 give us about the duration of our sufferings?

20 What does this passage tell us about the purposes of God for our lives and the eventual outcome of our suffering? How can God's grace transform our suffering into something of value and beauty?

Remember, what is good for your sins is good for your sorrows. The grace of God—seen in His provision for our sinful condition as well as His strength to escort us through hardship—is always available. The following personal story from coauthor Tim Grissom illustrates the way God ministers grace to His hurting children.

> A few years ago, my personal study on the topic of grace coincided with an unusually painful journey for my family and me.
>
> In January 1999, my wife, Janiece, was diagnosed with Amyotrophic Lateral Sclerosis (Lou Gehrig's disease). Over a span of eleven months, she deteriorated physically to where she could do little for herself beyond breathing, speaking faintly, and swallowing. Finally we had to hospitalize her; she died ten days later at the age of forty-one. I was left with four children, and a broken heart.
>
> That describes the earthly reality of our circumstances. Painful. Dreadful. Overwhelming.
>
> But there is another side—a heavenly side—where I found hope. I discovered that it is entirely possible to "walk through the valley of the shadow of death" while "fearing no evil." I learned that in the harshest of life's seasons we can actually grow in our awareness of God's presence. God can become so large in our understanding that other "realities" slip into the background. He offers Himself—His love, His companionship, His strength... His grace!
>
> As I passed through the months of my wife's illness and death, people often asked, "How are you?" I could only reply that I felt as if we were being covered and carried by God—that He was escorting us through the grief and protecting us from being mortally wounded by it.

When we are humble, God places His hands above us to cover us and beneath us to carry us.

About six months after Janiece died, I was reading in 1 Peter 5 when God drew my attention to verses 6 and 7: "Humble yourselves, therefore, under God's mighty hand, that he may lift you up in due time. Cast all your anxiety on him because he cares for you."

When we are humble, do you see where God places His hands? Above us to cover us and beneath us to carry us. Sometimes our humility comes via repentance from sin, and sometimes it comes through the pain of suffering. In either case, humility hails the presence of God, and He cups us in His hands. What better place to be?

21 What does Tim's experience reveal about the heart and ways of God that could be helpful to you or a friend who is going through a time of sorrow or hardship?

Day 4

Day 5: Making It Personal

Grace is one of the richest theological themes in the Bible. But it is far more than just a nice theoretical concept. The grace of God is a vital, practical, transforming gift that is available to every child of God, for every situation and circumstance and moment of life. Today we want to go a step further in applying what we have learned about the grace of God in this lesson by asking two questions: *What do we need God's grace for?* and *How can we get more of God's grace in our lives?*

> "Nothing whatever pertaining to godliness and real holiness can be accomplished without grace."
>
> —Augustine

What do we need God's grace for?

The correct answer is: *everything!* From birth to regeneration through sanctification, all the way to ultimate glorification—from the cradle to the grave—we are utterly, absolutely, entirely, always dependent on His grace! God's grace is His all-sufficient provision for every need we will ever have.

God's grace rushes to the scene of our *weakness and need.* Take a few moments to identify some specific ways that you need God's grace at this season of your life. Check any of the following that apply:

I need God's grace in my life to...

- ❍ deal with a major disappointment
- ❍ forgive someone who has hurt me deeply
- ❍ seek forgiveness from someone I have wronged
- ❍ mend a broken relationship
- ❍ break off a wrong relationship
- ❍ meet pressing financial needs
- ❍ handle loneliness
- ❍ deal with the pain of my past
- ❍ deal with the guilt and failure of my past
- ❍ be morally pure
- ❍ respond to a tough situation at work
- ❍ bear chronic physical pain
- ❍ repent of a particular sin
- ❍ resist a particular temptation
- ❍ overcome a besetting sin
- ❍ break a habit
- ❍ guard my tongue

- ❍ love a family member who is hard to love
- ❍ be faithful to my mate
- ❍ take a specific step of obedience
- ❍ honor my parents (or my in-laws)
- ❍ love my wife as Christ loves the church
- ❍ respect and submit to my husband
- ❍ be kind and patient with my kids
- ❍ accept a particular ministry opportunity
- ❍ fulfill the ministry He has entrusted to me

List any other circumstances that come to mind for which you need God's grace:

How can we get more of God's grace in our lives?

God's grace is undeserved, but it is not unconditional. God makes grace available, and He is eager to give it, but there is one condition that must be met.

> *But He gives more grace. Therefore it says, "God opposes the proud, but gives grace to the humble."* (James 4:6)

Insight

Both James and Peter (1 Peter 5:5) quote Proverbs 3:34—"Surely He scorns the scornful, but gives grace to the humble" (NKJV).

What kind of people does God oppose? Why?

What is God's condition for receiving more grace?

God resists (literally, "sets Himself against") those who are self-sufficient—those who try to manage their lives without Him; those who struggle and strive to live the Christian life on their own; those who are too proud to acknowledge their need.

But He gladly, freely lavishes His grace—all His divine favor and resources—on those who are humble. We demonstrate humility by acknowledging our helplessness and our need (to Him and to others) and by crying out to Him for His grace.

Read Psalm 84:11, James 1:17, and 1 Peter 5:10. What (Who!) is the source of all grace? What does that suggest about where we should look to get our needs met?

Look back at the items you checked for which you need God's grace right now. Humble yourself before the Lord and tell Him about each of those areas where you need His help. Call out to Him to meet your need. Then thank Him that *His grace is sufficient for you* in each of those areas.

Seeking Him **Together**

> "This one word 'grace' contains within itself the whole of New Testament theology."
>
> —J. I. Packer

Opening It Up

1. How would you define the concept of grace to a six-year-old?

2. How has your understanding of grace been helped or challenged this week?

Talking It Over

3. In the Faith-Builder story, how did it help the man to admit his "secret sins" to his wife? Did it also help her? How?

4. What were the risks of such honesty? Were the results worth the risks?

5. How does grace differ from justice? From mercy?

6. Explain how we see God's grace in salvation.

7. How can God's grace help us overcome temptation and deal with sin?

8. Read Hebrews 4:15–16 aloud. What insights does this passage give us about how to get more of God's grace?

9. We have seen that God resists the proud but gives grace to the humb (1 Peter 5:5–7). Why do you think that is true? What are some ways we humble ourselves and receive more of His grace?

"If left to ourselves, our sins will be too hard for us; but God's grace shall be sufficient to subdue them, so that they shall not rule us, and then they shall not ruin us."

—Matthew Henry

"Your worst days are never so bad that you're beyond the reach of God's grace. And your

Seeking Him Together

10. On Day 5, you were asked to indicate some of the things in your life for which you need God's grace. Go around the room and have each person share in a sentence one area in his life where he currently needs God's grace. One at a time, after each individual shares, have the group reassure that person by saying aloud together: *"His grace is sufficient for you."* Then have that person express faith by responding aloud: *"His grace is sufficient for me."*

Praying for Revival

Break up into groups of two, preferably with your previous prayer partner. Share any additional situations in your life where you are presently in need of God's grace. If you are struggling with unresolved sin issues, be as honest as you can with your partner. Remember, God pours grace on the humble. If you need more of God's grace (the desire and the power to obey Him), this is an opportunity for you to meet His condition of humility.

Pray together. Confess your need and cry out to God for His grace to meet that need. Pray that your partner will experience God's supernatural power in his/her life. Thank God for His saving, transforming, enabling, sustaining grace.

Lesson 6

Holiness:

A Heart Like His

The concept of *holiness* often conjures up images of dour faces, rigid rules, and self-righteousness. But seeking God and experiencing personal revival is anything but dull! So what does it mean to be holy?

Holiness can be defined on two levels. *Positional holiness* is what God imparts to us when we become His children. Since God is holy and we are sinners, we are reconciled to God by the blood of Christ shed on the cross (Colossians 1:19–22). God imparts Christ's righteousness to us and makes us holy and blameless before Him. That's our spiritual position in Christ. We have been separated from sin and set apart to God.

Personal holiness (or practical holiness), on the other hand, is the outworking and fruit of positional holiness, evidenced in the way we think and live. Because we belong to God and His Holy Spirit indwells us, we are commanded and divinely equipped to live according to His will every day, in every way. In this lesson, we will focus primarily on our practical, personal holiness.

"Strive for peace with everyone and for the holiness without which no one will see the Lord." (Hebrews 12:14)

Psalm 99
Ephesians 1:3–4; 5:25–27
1 Peter 1:13–17; 2:9–12

Day 1: **Faith-Builder Story**

1. What qualities come to mind when you think of *holiness?*

The following is a story of one man's experience of personal revival. Read what happened when he got a fresh glimpse of God's holiness.

> As a Christian and a pastor, I honestly believed that I had a righteous respect and reverence for the holiness of God. I often preached on God's holiness. But I had been hiding something for years. In my journal I often wrote about a struggle with a "secret sin." I never named the sin because I did not want to risk anyone discovering what was going on inside of me. But I knew what it was: I had a desperately impure thought life.
>
> One night God began to put His finger on this secret sin. I finally admitted to the Lord openly and honestly that I had been covering up this area of my life. Like so many men, I rationalized and justified it as part of being male. Yet I knew that what I was experiencing was more than just temptation. I had crossed the line. I had embraced immorality in my heart.

"One night God began to put His finger on this secret sin."

> I went to the Lord—broken, humbled, and repentant. And for the first time in many years I began to experience freedom in my life. The next day I shared with my wife what I had confessed to God. I sought her forgiveness as well, for I had not honored her in my thought life. She lovingly forgave me. Then I asked her to hold me accountable and periodically ask me about what I watched on television or what I read.

"For the first time in many years I began to experience freedom in my life."

> In Isaiah 6, the prophet Isaiah was confronted by the holiness of God. He cried, "Woe is me! For I am lost; for I am a man of unclean lips, and I dwell in the midst of a people of unclean lips; for my eyes have seen the King, the Lord of hosts!" As I realized anew the utter holiness of our God, I too was confronted with my own sinfulness. I knew I needed to share with my congregation what God had done in my life. So I preached from Isaiah 6 the next Sunday.
>
> With knees knocking and clammy hands, I told the congregation about my years of being entangled in thoughts of impurity. I asked them to forgive me. I was beginning to experience a wonderful freedom from

the bondage I had known for years, and I gave all the glory and honor to God.

I longed for others to know this freedom, so I invited any men who were also struggling in their thought life to join me in our chapel. I hoped maybe three or four men might join me to pray. Imagine my shock at seeing sixty-five men file through the door! Sixty-five of us, many with tears rolling down our cheeks, stood in a circle and began to confess to one another how we had failed to maintain purity in our thought life. I would not take anything for that precious moment when my brothers in Christ rallied around me and together we pledged ourselves to be accountable to one another, to pray for one another, to challenge one another.

When confronted with His holiness and our sinfulness, God lovingly begins to make us into what He wanted us to be all along: holy and pure vessels.

2 How did an awareness of God's holiness impact this man and his congregation?

3 The passage God used to convict this pastor's heart is a familiar one. Read Isaiah 6:1–7 thoughtfully, asking God to reveal Himself to you in a fresh way. As you read, imagine yourself in this scene. What do you think it would be like to truly experience the awesome presence of a holy God as Isaiah did? How does Isaiah's experience give you hope?

Day 1

Day 2: Truth Encounter

GETTING READY FOR THE WEDDING

Picture this scene. It's a perfect summer day. Friends and family have gathered to share in the joyful occasion. The decorations are elegant, and the mood is festive. Today you, the groom, will marry the woman of your dreams! Your thoughts are interrupted as the pipe organ sounds the wedding march. The congregation stands and turns to face the beautiful bride who is about to enter.

Then . . . a collective gasp. The bride clumsily staggers in with curlers in her hair and dressed in sweatpants. She looks in horror at the scene before her, and suddenly the meaning of it all sinks in. "I'm *soooo* sorry," she wails. "I forgot what today was!"

Sounds ridiculous, doesn't it? What bride has ever forgotten her wedding day or not actively prepared for it? However, among many Christians today we observe an even greater absurdity. In Scripture, the church (comprised of all who have been born into God's family through repentance and faith in Christ) is referred to as Christ's "bride" (Revelation 19:7; 21:2, 9; 22:17). The Lord Jesus Himself has promised to return to take His bride to the home He is preparing in heaven. At that time, there will be a great wedding feast and celebration.

The apostle Paul gives us a moving description of our heavenly Bridegroom's heart for His bride and His express desire for the wedding day yet to come:

> [25] *Christ loved the church and gave himself up for her,* [26] *that he might sanctify her, having cleansed her by the washing of water with the word,* [27] *so that he might present the church to himself in splendor, without spot or wrinkle or any such thing, that she might be holy and without blemish.* (Ephesians 5:25–27)

Insight

To be sanctified is to be made holy in our practice. Sanctification is a process that begins in every child of God at the point of regeneration and continues until our final glorification when we see Christ face-to-face.

4 According to this passage, why did Jesus die, and what is His objective for His bride, the church?

Sadly, many Christians today live as if they've forgotten about the wedding. In one sense, *revival* could be defined as "the bride getting ready for the wedding"! It is the church (which includes every true believer) preparing to meet her Bridegroom by becoming holy—cleansed of all that defiles. If this is the intent of our Savior for His bride, should it not also be the life-long focus and motivation of every child of God?

Key Point 

The Lord Jesus gave His life to make us a pure bride.

5 How important is "getting ready for the wedding" in your thinking and daily life?

- ❍ Truthfully, I am pretty much preoccupied with life here and now; I don't spend much time or focus on becoming holy or getting ready to meet Christ.
- ❍ I give some thought and effort to becoming holy and preparing for Christ's return, but often find myself distracted and consumed with things of this earth.
- ❍ I love the Lord Jesus, am excited about His return, and am actively seeking to "get ready for the wedding" by pursuing holiness.

Though we don't know when Christ will return, the Scripture tells us how to live now in preparation for our heavenly inheritance:

> [13]*Therefore, preparing your minds for action, and being sober-minded, set your hope fully on the grace that will be brought to you at the revelation of Jesus Christ.* [14]*As obedient children, do not be conformed to the passions of your former ignorance,* [15]*but as he who called you is holy, you also be holy in all your conduct,* [16]*since it is written, "You shall be holy, for I am holy."* (1 Peter 1:13–16)

Insight 

The word *holy* means "set apart." Personal holiness means to be separated from sin and consecrated to God for His purposes and His use.

6 What instructions does Peter give those awaiting Christ's return?

Day 2

7 Why are we to be holy? How are we to show it?

Language can be either passive or active. Passive language refers to something that is being done for us or to us. Active language describes the action we take to cause something to happen or to prevent something from happening.

8 What type of language—passive or active—is used in 1 Peter 1:13–16? What does that tell you about holiness?

! Key Point

We must actively cooperate with God in order to be holy.

Many other Scriptures make clear that we have a personal responsibility when it comes to holiness. For example:

- *Keep yourself pure* (1 Timothy 5:22).
- *Awake to righteousness, and sin not* (1 Corinthians 15:34).
- *Let every one that names the name of the Lord depart from iniquity* (2 Timothy 2:19).
- *Abhor what is evil; cling to what is good* (Romans 12:9).
- *Let us cleanse ourselves from all defilement of body and spirit, bringing holiness to completion in the fear of God* (2 Corinthians 7:1).

God has commanded us to be holy. Our motivation is to be like Him and to prepare for His return. But personal holiness is not something we passively wait for God to mystically bestow on us. We must actively cooperate with Him in order to become holy in "all our conduct."

Maybe you're thinking, *I really want to be holy, but I keep failing! It seems so impossible!* Remember…God would not command us to do anything that He will not enable us to do. If you are a child of God, He has given you His Holy Spirit to help you in the life-long process of sanctification. God's grace will give you the desire and the power to pursue holiness in every area of your life (Philippians 2:13).

At the end of 1 Thessalonians, after challenging the believers to live holy lives, the apostle Paul encourages them with this benediction:

> 23*Now may the God of peace himself sanctify you completely, and may your whole spirit and soul and body be kept blameless at the coming of our Lord Jesus Christ.* 24*He who calls you is faithful; he will surely do it.* (1 Thessalonians 4:23–24)

9 How do these verses give you hope in relation to the process of your sanctification?

10 Write a brief prayer expressing your desire to pursue holiness and to be ready to meet your Bridegroom. Ask for His grace to enable you to obey, and thank Him for His promise and His power to make you holy.

Day 2

Day 3: Truth Encounter

THE HEART OF THE MATTER

! Key Point

True holiness is foremost a matter of the heart.

The religious leaders of Jesus' day were greatly respected and were considered by all (including themselves!) to be "holy." They were experts in the Old Testament law. They prided themselves on keeping the law down to the smallest letter. Their outward behavior could not be faulted. Imagine their consternation when Jesus appeared on the scene and began to confront them over the one thing no one but God could see: *their hearts.*

Here is just one example of many encounters Jesus had with these leaders who thought they were "holy":

> *1Now when the Pharisees gathered to him, with some of the scribes who had come from Jerusalem, 2they saw that some of his disciples ate with hands that were defiled, that is, unwashed. 3(For the Pharisees and all the Jews do not eat unless they wash their hands, holding to the tradition of the elders, 4and when they come from the marketplace, they do not eat unless they wash. And there are many other traditions that they observe, such as the washing of cups and pots and copper vessels and dining couches.)*
>
> *5And the Pharisees and the scribes asked him, "Why do your disciples not walk according to the tradition of the elders, but eat with defiled hands?" 6And he said to them, "Well did Isaiah prophesy of you hypocrites, as it is written, 'This people honors me with their lips, but their heart is far from me; 7in vain do they worship me, teaching as doctrines the commandments of men.' 8You leave the commandment of God and hold to the tradition of men."* (Mark 7:1–8)

Insight

Over the centuries Jewish religious leaders had added a large body of rules ("the traditions of the elders") to the Old Testament law. Among these rules were precise regulations about how to wash one's hands, even prescribing how much water to use and how to pour it.

11 What did the disciples do (or not do) that disturbed the Pharisees? Why did this bother them?

12 What did Jesus call the Pharisees (v. 6)? Why did He use such a strong term (vv. 6–8)?

Matthew 23 records another occasion on which Jesus strongly rebuked the Pharisees for their hypocrisy. Among other things, He accused them of:

- not practicing what they preached to others (v. 3)
- doing their "spiritual" deeds in order to make a good impression on others (vv. 5–7)

Further, Jesus said, there was a world of difference between what they *appeared* to be (based on outward evidence) and what they actually were (based on the inward reality):

> [25]*"Woe to you, scribes and Pharisees, hypocrites! For you clean the outside of the cup and the plate, but inside they are full of greed and self-indulgence....*[28] *So you also outwardly appear righteous to others, but within you are full of hypocrisy and lawlessness."* (vv. 25, 28)

The Pharisees' *hearts* (what God knew was on the inside) did not match up to all their impressive "spiritual" *talk* and *behavior.* They were scrupulously "clean" on the outside, but they were corrupt on the inside. They were *hypocrites.* They made up their own rules and traditions, exalted them above the Word of God, and considered themselves godly because they conformed (outwardly) to their man-made standards. They kept certain laws meticulously (e.g., tithing everything, including their spices!), while managing to bypass the heart behind the laws (e.g., truly loving God and others).

On the face of things, the behavior of someone who is genuinely holy (not perfect, but living in humble obedience to God) and someone who is a hypocrite may seem quite similar. But God doesn't look on the face of things; He looks at our hearts. He doesn't just *glance* at our hearts; He *searches* them.

13 Take some moments to let God search your heart. Reflect on these questions and record anything God puts on your heart:

Does Jesus' description of the Pharisees apply to your life in any way? In what way?

As God searches your heart, what does He see, true holiness or hypocrisy? Are you really as spiritual as others think you are? Or are you a hypocrite—someone who just *looks* and *acts* spiritual? Is the impression others have of you consistent with what God knows to be the real condition of your heart?

14 Write a brief prayer confessing any hypocrisy God may have shown you in your heart and asking Him to give you a pure heart.

Day 4: Truth Encounter

SUFFERING GRACE

Write one or two words that come to mind when you hear the following words:

Candy: ______

Sunset: ______

Bride: ______

Now, write a few words that come to your mind when you hear the word *holiness:*

Did your list include the words *gladness* or *joy*? Surprising as it may seem, *holiness* and *gladness* really do go hand in hand.

In Psalm 4, David talks about two kinds of people: the *godly*—those who love righteousness, and the *ungodly*—those who are drawn to sin.

> [1] *Answer me when I call, O God of my righteousness!*
> *You have given me relief when I was in distress.*
> *Be gracious to me and hear my prayer!*
> [2] *O men, how long shall my honor be turned into shame?*
> *How long will you love vain words and seek after lies? Selah*
> [3] *But know that the Lord has set apart the godly for himself;*
> *the Lord hears when I call to him.*
> [4] *Be angry, and do not sin;*
> *ponder in your own hearts on your beds, and be silent. Selah*
> [5] *Offer right sacrifices,*
> *and put your trust in the Lord.*

15 What characteristics of ungodly people do you see in this passage (v. 2)?

> "Holiness is a most beautiful and lovely thing. We drink in strange notions of holiness from our childhood, as if it were a melancholy, morose, sour and unpleasant thing; but there is nothing in it but what is sweet and ravishingly lovely."
>
> —Jonathan Edwards

Day 4

16 In contrast to the ungodly, David professes his love for holiness and his earnest intent to be pleasing to God. What are some characteristics of godly people found in verses 1, 3–5?

By choosing the pathway of holiness, David sometimes found himself under attack. Yet, David didn't feel sorry for himself; he wasn't miserable or depressed. Notice how he describes his condition:

> *You have put more joy in my heart than they have when their grain and wine abound.* (v. 7)

17 According to David's experience, what is the result of loving holiness and rejecting sin?

Psalm 32 records for us David's personal testimony after he fell into horrible sin and then repented and received God's great mercy:

> 1 ***Blessed** is the one whose transgression is forgiven,*
> *whose sin is covered.*
> 2 ***Blessed** is the man against whom the Lord counts no iniquity,*
> *and in whose spirit there is no deceit.* (vv. 1–2; emphasis added)

18 When we sin, we do so because we think it will bring us some sort of pleasure. What did David discover about the way to experience true blessing?

Insight

In Hebrews 1:9, the writer is actually quoting Psalm 45:7, a messianic prophecy that points to Christ.

The fruit of holiness is *gladness* and *joy*! The Scripture gives us a description of the Lord Jesus that makes this connection:

> *You have loved righteousness and hated wickedness; therefore God, your God, has anointed you with the oil of gladness beyond your companions.* (Hebrews 1:9)

The perspective of Satan, the world, and our natural mind-set is the polar opposite of God's way of thinking. They try to convince us that:

If you choose to be holy, you will feel ____________ ; and

If you want to be happy, you need to ____________ .

19 What do you learn from the example of David and Jesus about the true pathway to gladness and joy?

> "Man's holiness is now his greatest happiness, and in heaven, man's greatest happiness will be his perfect holiness."
>
> —Thomas Brooks

Day 4

Day5: Making It Personal

In several of his epistles, the apostle Paul shares an important insight about the life-long process of pursuing holiness:

> [22]*Put off your old self, which belongs to your former manner of life and is corrupt through deceitful desires, and…* [23] *be renewed in the spirit of your minds, and…*[24] *put on the new self, created after the likeness of God in true righteousness and holiness.* (Ephesians 4:22–24)

As "new creatures" in Christ, we are to "put off" anything and everything that is a part of our old, corrupt flesh—sinful habits, wrong attitudes, impure motives, and so on. But it's not enough just to "put off" the old life. In its place, by God's grace and by the power of His Holy Spirit, we must actively "put on the new self"—those qualities of the life of Christ within us.

Below is a list of some things every child of God needs to "put off," along with corresponding qualities we are to "put on" in their place. Prayerfully read through the entire list and *put a check next to each item that God reveals you have a particular need to "put off."* Don't hurry through this exercise—ask God to use it to reveal specific areas in your life that are not holy.

When you are finished, spend time alone with God in confession and prayer, using this list as a guide. In the days ahead, take time to read and meditate on the Scripture verses that relate to the items you have checked, and begin to put on the contrasting qualities in their place.

Put off...	Put on...
❍ 1. Lack of love (1 John 4:7–8, 20)	❍ 1. Love (John 15:12)
❍ 2. Judging (Matt. 7:1–2)	❍ 2. Let God search my heart (John 8:9; 15:22)
❍ 3. Bitterness, unforgiveness (Heb. 12:15)	❍ 3. Tenderhearted, forgiving (Eph. 4:32)
❍ 4. Selfishness (Phil. 2:21)	❍ 4. Self-denial (John 12:24)
❍ 5. Pride (Prov. 16:5)	❍ 5. Humility (James 4:6)
❍ 6. Boasting or conceit (1 Cor. 4:7)	❍ 6. Esteeming others (Phil. 2:3)

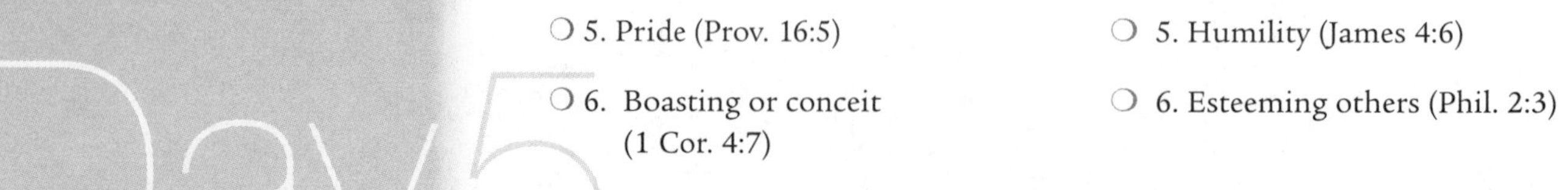

Put off...	Put on...
❍ 7. Stubbornness (1 Sam. 15:23)	❍ 7. Brokenness (Rom. 6:13)
❍ 8. Disrespect for authority (Acts 23:5)	❍ 8. Honor authority (Heb. 13:17)
❍ 9. Rebellion (1 Sam. 15:23)	❍ 9. Submission (Heb. 13:17)
❍ 10. Disobedience (1 Sam. 12:15)	❍ 10. Obedience (Deut. 11:27)
❍ 11. Impatience (James 1:2–4)	❍ 11. Patience (Heb. 10:36)
❍ 12. Ungratefulness (Rom. 1:21)	❍ 12. Gratitude (Col. 3:15–17)
❍ 13. Covetousness (Luke 12:15)	❍ 13. Contentment (Heb. 13:5)
❍ 14. Discontentment (Heb. 13:5)	❍ 14. Contentment (1 Tim. 6:8)
❍ 15. Murmuring, complaining (Phil. 2:14)	❍ 15. Praise (Heb. 13:15)
❍ 16. Jealousy (Gal. 5:26)	❍ 16. Trust (1 Cor. 13:4)
❍ 17. Strife, contention (Prov. 13:10)	❍ 17. Peace (James 3:17)
❍ 18. Retaliation (Prov. 24:29)	❍ 18. Return good for evil (Rom. 12:19–20)
❍ 19. Anger (Prov. 29:22)	❍ 19. Self-control (Gal. 5:22–23)
❍ 20. Wrath (James 1:19–20)	❍ 20. Soft answer (Prov. 15:1)
❍ 21. Easily irritated (1 Cor. 13:5)	❍ 21. Not easily provoked (Prov. 19:11)
❍ 22. Hatred (Matt. 5:21–22)	❍ 22. Love (1 Cor. 13:3)
❍ 23. Gossip (1 Tim. 5:13)	❍ 23. Edifying speech (Eph. 4:29)
❍ 24. Evil speaking (James 4:11)	❍ 24. Good report (Prov. 15:30)
❍ 25. Critical spirit (Gal. 5:15)	❍ 25. Kindness (Col. 3:12)
❍ 26. Lying (Eph. 4:25)	❍ 26. Speaking the truth (Zech. 8:16)
❍ 27. Profanity (Prov. 4:24)	❍ 27. Pure speech (Prov. 15:4)
❍ 28. Idle words (Matt. 12:36)	❍ 28. Words that minister grace (Eph. 4:29)

"Sin tastes sweet but turns bitter in our stomachs. Holiness often tastes bitter but turns sweet in our stomachs."

—Gary Thomas

Day 5

Put off...	Put on...
❍ 29. Wrong motives (1 Sam. 16:7)	❍ 29. Spiritual motives (1 Cor. 10:31)
❍ 30. Evil thoughts (Matt. 15:19)	❍ 30. Pure thoughts (Phil. 4:8)
❍ 31. Complacency (Rev. 3:15)	❍ 31. Zeal (Rev. 3:19)
❍ 32. Slothfulness (Prov. 18:9)	❍ 32. Diligence (Prov. 6:6–11)
❍ 33. Hypocrisy (Job 8:13)	❍ 33. Sincerity (1 Thess. 2:3)
❍ 34. Idolatry (Deut. 11:16)	❍ 34. Worshiping God only (Col. 1:18)
❍ 35. Left first love (Rev. 2:4)	❍ 35. Fervent devotion (Rev. 2:5)
❍ 36. Lack of rejoicing always (Phil. 4:4)	❍ 36. Rejoicing (1 Thess. 5:18)
❍ 37. Worry, fear (Matt. 6:25–32)	❍ 37. Trust (1 Peter 5:7)
❍ 38. Unbelief (Heb. 3:12)	❍ 38. Faith (Heb. 11:1, 6)
❍ 39. Neglect of Bible study (2 Tim. 3:14–17)	❍ 39. Bible study, meditation (Ps. 1:2)
❍ 40. Prayerlessness (Luke 18:1)	❍ 40. Praying (Matt. 26:41)
❍ 41. No burden for the lost (Matt. 9:36–38)	❍ 41. Compassion, witnessing (Acts 1:8)
❍ 42. Procrastination (Prov. 10:5)	❍ 42. Diligence (Prov. 27:1)
❍ 43. Inhospitability (1 Peter 4:9)	❍ 43. Hospitality (Rom. 12:13)
❍ 44. Cheating (2 Cor. 4:2)	❍ 44. Honesty (2 Cor. 8:21)
❍ 45. Stealing (Prov. 29:24)	❍ 45. Working, giving (Eph. 4:28)
❍ 46. Lack of moderation (Prov. 11:1)	❍ 46. Temperance (1 Cor. 9:25)
❍ 47. Gluttony (Prov. 23:21)	❍ 47. Discipline (1 Cor. 9:27)
❍ 48. Wrong friends (Ps. 1:1)	❍ 48. Godly friends (Prov. 13:20)
❍ 49. Temporal values (Matt. 6:19–21)	❍ 49. Eternal values (2 Cor. 4:18)

"Those who tolerate sin in what they think to be little things, will soon indulge it in greater matters."

—C. H. Spurgeon

Day 5

Put off...	Put on...
❍ 50. Love of money, greed (1 Tim. 6:9–10)	❍ 50. Love of God (Matt. 6:33)
❍ 51. Stinginess (1 John 3:17)	❍ 51. Generosity (Prov. 11:25)
❍ 52. Moral impurity (1 Thess. 4:7)	❍ 52. Moral purity (1 Thess. 4:4)
❍ 53. Fornication (1 Cor. 6:18)	❍ 53. Abstinence (1 Thess. 4:3)
❍ 54. Lust (1 Peter 2:11)	❍ 54. Pure desires (Titus 2:12)
❍ 55. Adultery (Matt. 5:27–28)	❍ 55. Marital fidelity (Prov. 5:15–20)
❍ 56. Pornography (Ps. 101:3)	❍ 56. Pure thoughts (Phil. 4:8)
❍ 57. Immodest dress (Prov. 7:10)	❍ 57. Modesty (1 Tim. 2:9)
❍ 58. Flirtation (Prov. 7:21)	❍ 58. Gentle, quiet spirit (1 Peter 3:4)
❍ 59. Worldly entertainment (Prov. 21:17)	❍ 59. Spiritual pursuits (Gal. 5:16)
❍ 60. Bodily harm (1 Cor. 3:16–17)	❍ 60. Glorifying God in my body (1 Cor. 6:20)
❍ 61. Drunkenness (Prov. 20:1)	❍ 61. Sobriety (Prov. 23:30–32)
❍ 62. Following the crowd (Prov. 1:10)	❍ 62. God-fearing (Prov. 3:7)
❍ 63. Witchcraft, astrology, horoscopes (Deut. 18:10–12)	❍ 63. Worship of God (Deut. 6:5)
❍ 64. Gambling (Prov. 28:20, 22)	❍ 64. Good stewardship (Luke 16:11)
❍ 65. Preferential treatment (James 2:1–9)	❍ 65. Loving neighbor as self (Luke 6:27–36) [1]

[1] This list is from a handout published by Life Action Ministries, © 1982. Used by permission. For a printable version of the complete list, visit www.LifeAction.org.

Seeking Him **Together**

Opening It Up

1. Who do you know (or know of) who has lived what you consider a holy life? Explain your answer.

Talking It Over

2. Define "positional holiness" and "personal holiness." What's the difference between the two?

3. Why do you think the pastor in the Faith-Builder story felt it was necessary to confess his "secret sin" to his wife? to his church?

4. What effect did his humble confession have on others? Have you seen any "ripples of revival" in others' lives recently, as you have been responding to God through the course of this study?

"Holiness is not something we are called upon to do in order that we may become something; it is something we are to do because of what we already are."

—Martyn Lloyd-Jones

5. Review the illustration (Day 2) of the bride forgetting her wedding day. Do you see any similarities between that bride and the current condition of the bride of Christ? How should knowing that Christ will return for His "bride" affect the way we think and live?

6. First Peter 1:13–16 and other Scriptures urge us to be active in our pursuit of holiness. How can we cooperate with God to grow in personal holiness?

7. Why was Jesus so "hard" on the Pharisees, when everyone else thought they were model "believers"?

8. Take turns reading aloud the following list of comparative statements about the difference between hypocrites and people who are truly holy.

- **Holy people** behave in certain ways because they love God.
- **Hypocrites** behave in certain ways because they want others to think they love God.

- **Holy people** are concerned about being pleasing to God—inside and out.
- **Hypocrites** are concerned about how they are perceived by others.

"Christian holiness is not a matter of painstaking conformity to the individual precepts of an external law code; it is rather a question of the Holy Spirit's producing His fruit in the life, reproducing those graces which were seen in perfection in the life of Christ."

—F. F. Bruce

Seeking Him Together

- **Holy people** have a heart to love and serve others, regardless of their socioeconomic status.
- **Hypocrites** like to associate with "movers and shakers" and the "up-and-coming," to enhance their own standing.

- **Holy people** bow to the authority of Scripture and live radically obedient lives.
- **Hypocrites** will excuse disobedience to the Word of God through use of pious-sounding logic, while slavishly adhering to their own man-made rules and standards.

- **Holy people** give themselves unreservedly to God and are patient with others who are still in process.
- **Hypocrites** expect more from others than they are willing to give of themselves.

- **Holy people** have a humble estimation of themselves because God is their standard.
- **Hypocrites** compare themselves to others and develop a spiritual superiority complex.

- **Holy people** base their convictions on the standard of God's Word.
- **Hypocrites** exalt personal preferences and human traditions to a position of equal (or greater) authority with the Word of God.

- **Holy people** are real.
- **Hypocrites** pretend...
  to do things they don't.
  to abstain from things they do.
  to love things they hate.
  to hate things they love.
  to want things they dread.
  to dread things they want.

Do you see yourself in any of the statements describing hypocrites? If you feel the freedom to do so, share what God has been showing you about any hypocrisy in your life.

9. How can believers be delivered from hypocrisy and move toward living more authentically holy lives?

10. How did the Lord use the "Put Off/Put On" exercise in your heart? What are some practical ways you can continue to put off the "old self" and put on the "new self"?

Praying for Revival

Break into pairs for prayer. Tell your prayer partner at least one area of personal revival—humility, repentance, honesty, grace, personal holiness—that God is dealing with you about; then pray for each other.

Pray too for a revival of true holiness in the church today. Pray for a restoration of personal and corporate purity; pray that the bride of Christ will become committed to "getting ready for the wedding."

For further encouragement and accountability, call each other during the week to discuss what you are learning as you seek the Lord and how you are responding to His Spirit.

Lesson 7

Obedience: The Acid Test of Love

God loves His children. He knows that we cannot fully experience and enjoy His love unless we are obedient to Him. Obeying God is not meant to be a sterile, cold requirement; rather, it is a willing, gladhearted response to One who loves us extravagantly and has our best interests at heart. God does not stand by at a distance, demanding our obedience. Rather, He blesses us by allowing us to be a part of accomplishing His purposes. He calls us to surrender, invites us to follow, empowers us to serve, and then blesses our obedience.

"If you love me, you will keep my commandments." **(John 14:15)**

Deuteronomy 30:11–20
Psalm 119:57–64
Philippians 2:5–11
1 John 2:3–6; 5:1–5

Day 1: Faith-Builder Story

1 What comes to mind when you think of the concept of obedience? Is it a positive or negative concept to you? Why?

Read the following story about the lessons one businessman learned in God's school of obedience.

> *"This was more than improved business ethics; it was vital to walking with God in total obedience."*

I didn't think much was wrong in my life. I was the president of a growing furniture manufacturing company. I had a great family and served as a deacon in my church. I was respected in the community. So when our pastor asked the deacons to pray about inviting a team to our church for a revival crusade, I wasn't convinced of the need. But I soon found out that God always looks deeper than we do.

During the services, God searched my heart and revealed things that fell short of His glory. One specific issue involved some business practices. In the furniture industry it is common practice to duplicate (as nearly as possible) the successful designs of other companies. I had recently done this twice without thinking anything about it. However, under the scrutiny of Scripture and the Holy Spirit, I saw this practice as God saw it—dishonest. Even though it was accepted, I could no longer excuse the practice of stealing competitors' designs.

After confessing this sin to God, I knew that the next step was to call the men whose designs I had copied, ask their forgiveness, and commit to making financial restitution. To me, this was more than improved business ethics; it was vital to walking with God in total obedience. I made the calls; the first man appreciated the call but declined any financial reimbursement. His outlook was the same as mine used to be: "Forget about it. Everybody does it; it's really no big deal." The second man verbalized forgiveness and appreciation. He also declined financial reimbursement but suggested that my company donate the amount ($18,000) to a charity of our choice.

There were changes to be made at home as well. I realized that I had been a good provider but an absent husband and father. I was working far too many hours, and my family was suffering for it. I began to see

that God could take care of our needs and our business. I didn't need to be at the office all the time. So I cut back on work hours and invested that time at home.

God showed me that obedience, or the lack thereof, has a profound effect on interpersonal relationships. First and foremost, God wants our relationship with Him to be right. Before we ever try to give or do anything for God, His primary concern is for us to be right with Him. That requires total obedience. Once we are right with God, other relationships become what they need to be.

"Like so many areas in our walk with God, obedience requires a daily, if not moment-by-moment, surrender."

Even though I had encountered many lessons about obedience and the price of disobedience, I had occasional setbacks. Like so many areas in our walk with God, obedience requires a daily, if not moment-by-moment, surrender. About six years after the incident involving the copied furniture designs, our company accountant came to me with a dilemma. The government had neglected to charge tax on a duty transfer, an oversight that put the company ahead by $20,000. The accountant wanted to know what he should do about it. I said, "Let me think about it and get back to you in the morning." But I knew what we needed to do. There really wasn't anything to think or pray about. I called the guy first thing the next morning and apologized for not doing the right thing immediately. We owed the money, and there should never have been any question whether or not we would pay. When the choice between right and wrong is obvious, I have to obey God and do the right thing.

"God's way works! It's the best way to live."

I'm not perfect, by any means, but I do love the Lord and want to please Him. Earlier in my life, I was too concerned with how I appeared to others. If someone pointed out a problem in my life, I'd deal with just the branches, leaves, and fruits. But when God began to deal with me about total obedience, He got to the root of the matter. God's way works! Even if we didn't get eternal life, obeying God and living according to His values protects us. We could avoid so many struggles and hurts. It's definitely the best way to live.

2 What do you think he means when he says, "Obedience requires a daily, if not moment-by-moment, surrender"? How have you experienced this truth in your walk with God?

Read the following verses from Psalm 19:

> 7 *The law of the Lord is perfect,*
> *reviving the soul;*
> *the testimony of the Lord is sure,*
> *making wise the simple. . . .*
> 10 *More to be desired are they than gold,*
> *even much fine gold;*
> *sweeter also than honey*
> *and drippings of the honeycomb.*
> 11 *Moreover, by them is your servant warned;*
> *in keeping them there is great reward.*

3 According to this passage, what are some of the blessings ("rewards") of knowing and obeying God's Word?

Day 1

Day 2: **Truth Encounter**

THE FOUNDATION OF THE CHRISTIAN LIFE

When you were a child, you may have sung a little chorus called "The Wise Man Built His House upon the Rock." That song is taken from a parable in the gospel of Matthew, where Jesus explained the importance of building our lives on a firm foundation:

> 24 *Everyone then who hears these words of mine and does them will be like a wise man who built his house on the rock.* 25 *And the rain fell, and the floods came, and the winds blew and beat on that house, but it did not fall, because it had been founded on the rock.*
>
> 26 *And everyone who hears these words of mine and does not do them will be like a foolish man who built his house on the sand.* 27 *And the rain fell, and the floods came, and the winds blew and beat against that house, and it fell, and great was the fall of it.* (Matthew 7:24–27)

Insight 

In both the Old and New Testaments, the words translated *obey* are related to the idea of hearing. Obedience is a positive, active response to listening to the Word of God. Jesus said, "Blessed rather are those who hear the word of God and keep it" (Luke 11:28).

The lesson is quite simple. The wise person is *obedient* to the Word of the Lord. He chooses to build his life on hearing and doing the will of God. When trials and temptations assault him (as they will), he does not fall. He is secure because his foundation is solid. The foolish person, on the other hand, hears the Word of the Lord but does not act on it. He too is inundated with trouble at times and, having no foundation, he collapses.

Obedience is literally foundational to the Christian life. No obedience, no foundation. Unless we are living in obedience to what God says, we have nothing upon which to build our lives, nothing upon which to rest for assurance, and nothing to rely on when we are tested. Jesus said this is the way to be wise! Trust Him, follow Him, obey Him, and you will be building on a Rock.

Key Point 

Obedience is foundational to the Christian life.

4 Can you think of an example of how knowing and obeying Christ's words proved to be a solid foundation for your life during a time of testing or adversity?

The only reliable means of measuring our love for God is to examine whether we obey Him. We may dress the part, act the part, talk the part of being a Christian, but none of these things prove that we genuinely love God. Obedience is the only way.

Day 2

! Key Point

Obedience is the proof of our love for God.

5 Read the following verses, and circle the words *love(s)* and *keep(s)*.

> [21] *"Whoever has my commandments and keeps them, he it is who loves me. And he who loves me will be loved by my Father, and I will love him and manifest myself to him...."*
>
> [23] *Jesus answered him, "If anyone loves me, he will keep my word, and my Father will love him, and we will come to him and make our home with him.* [24] *Whoever does not love me does not keep my words. And the word that you hear is not mine but the Father's who sent me."* (John 14:21, 23–24)

6 Based on Jesus' statements above, mark the following statements **T** (true) or **F** (false).

_____ I can love God and not keep His commandments.
_____ If I love God, I will obey Him and keep His commandments.
_____ My obedience is a sign of my love for God.

Do you see the relationship between love and obedience? If you truly love God, you will seek to know and to keep His commands. If you are not keeping His commands, you cannot honestly claim to love Him. Actions speak louder than words.

7 When we obey God, we prove that we love Him. According to this passage, how does obeying God affect our capacity to know God and to experience His love for us?

8 Does your life give evidence that you love God? In what ways? Write out your thoughts.

Day 2

Day 3: Truth Encounter

OBEDIENCE AND GOD'S GLORY

There are countless examples in the Bible of people who obeyed and disobeyed God. Today let's look at Moses' life.

God gave Moses an enormous assignment: build the tabernacle (Exodus 25:1–9). God Himself designed this unusual portable structure that would become the centerpiece of Israel's culture and worship for centuries. He gave Moses a detailed "blueprint" and precise instructions regarding its construction. Moses was then responsible to see that the workers did everything exactly as God had directed.

The construction process took many months, unprecedented varieties and quantities of material, and the cooperation of every man and woman in the nation. When the job was completed, an awesome thing happened: *God's glory filled the tabernacle.* His manifest presence hovered in a way so glorious that no one, not even Moses, could stand to enter. The God of heaven visited earth!

Exodus 39–40 records the process of the making of the priestly garments and the tabernacle construction. Read these excerpts and *underline the key phrase that is repeated in each verse:*

> *[39][1] From the blue and purple and scarlet yarns they made finely*
> *woven garments, for ministering in the Holy Place. They made the holy*
> *garments for Aaron, as the Lord had commanded Moses.... [5] And the*
> *skillfully woven band on it was of one piece with it and made like it,*
> *of gold, blue and purple and scarlet yarns, and fine twined linen, as*
> *the Lord had commanded Moses.... [7] And he set them on the shoul-*
> *der pieces of the ephod to be stones of remembrance for the sons of*
> *Israel, as the Lord had commanded Moses.... [32] Thus all the work of the*
> *tabernacle of the tent of meeting was finished, and the people of Israel*
> *did according to all that the Lord had commanded Moses.... [43] Then*
> *Moses blessed them....*
> *[40] [19] He spread the tent over the tabernacle and put the covering*
> *of the tent over it, as the Lord had commanded Moses.... [21] And he*
> *brought the ark into the tabernacle and set up the veil of the screen,*
> *and screened the ark of the testimony, as the Lord had commanded*
> *Moses.... [23] and arranged the bread on it before the Lord, as the Lord*
> *had commanded Moses.... [25] and set up the lamps before the Lord,*
> *as the Lord had commanded Moses.... [27] and burned fragrant incense*
> *on it, as the Lord had commanded Moses.... [29] And he set the altar of*
> *burnt offering at the entrance of the tabernacle of the tent of meeting,*

Key Point 

If we want to see the glory of God in revival, we must obey God.

Insight 

The tabernacle was the place where God met with His people; it housed the manifest presence of God, which the Jews came to call the *shekinah* glory of God. (This Hebrew word actually is not found in the Bible.) It means, literally, *residence* or *dwelling.* Over time, it came to mean *God's visible presence.*

Day 3

and offered on it the burnt offering and the grain offering, as the Lord had commanded Moses.... [32] *When they went into the tent of meeting, and when they approached the altar, they washed, as the Lord commanded Moses.*

9 What key phrase did you underline? Why do you think God might have inspired that particular detail to be repeated so many times in this account? What does that phrase tell you about Moses and the children of Israel?

Now read Exodus 40:33–34:

[33] *So Moses finished the work.* [34] *Then the cloud covered the tent of meeting, and the glory of the Lord filled the tabernacle.*

10 Which of the following came first?

- God's glory filling the tabernacle
- complete obedience

11 What do you think is the significance of this order of events and of the fact that God's glory did not fall until the people had finished the work of obeying His instructions?

God's glory filled the tabernacle after months of obedience on the part of Moses and others. God chose to gloriously manifest Himself where His people had been faithful and obedient. In similar fashion, if we desire to see God's glory in revival and spiritual awakening in our day, we must return to Him in full obedience.

12 Write a prayer asking God to help you obey His commands and to manifest His glory in and through your life.

Day 4: Truth Encounter

SAUL THE HALF-HEARTED

The blessing of God came as Moses and the people of Israel fully obeyed. But God's servant-leaders were not always so submissive. Consider, for example, Saul, the first king of Israel.

Read the Scripture passages below and answer the corresponding questions.

> 1 *And Samuel said to Saul, "The Lord sent me to anoint you king*
> *over his people Israel; now therefore listen to the words of the Lord.*
> 2 *Thus says the Lord of hosts, 'I have noted what Amalek did to Israel*
> *in opposing them on the way when they came up out of Egypt.* 3 *Now*
> *go and strike Amalek and devote to destruction all that they have. Do not spare them, but kill both man and woman, child and infant, ox and sheep, camel and donkey.'"* (1 Samuel 15:1–3)

13 Whose word did Samuel speak to Saul? What, exactly, was Saul told to do?

> 5 *And Saul came to the city of Amalek and lay in wait in the valley....*
> 7 *And Saul defeated the Amalekites from Havilah as far as Shur, which*
> *is east of Egypt.* 8 *And he took Agag the king of the Amalekites alive*
> *and devoted to destruction all the people with the edge of the sword.*
> 9 *But Saul and the people spared Agag and the best of the sheep and of the oxen and of the fattened calves and the lambs, and all that was good, and would not utterly destroy them. All that was despised and worthless they devoted to destruction.* (1 Samuel 15:5, 7–9)

14 Did Saul obey God? Why or why not? (Support your answer.)

Key Point 

Partial obedience is disobedience.

Insight 

The Amalekites were descendants of Esau's grandson Amalek. They lived in the Sinai Peninsula and the Negev Desert south of Israel. They stood under God's judgment for their unprovoked attack on the Israelites in Moses's time (Exodus 17:8–16; Deuteronomy 25:17–19).

Day 4

Insight

Gilgal, a town located just north of Jericho in the Jordan River Valley, was the site of many important events in Israelite history. It seems to have been a worship center, and this was perhaps why Saul went there to offer a sacrifice. But because of his disobedience, Gilgal—which had been the site of Saul's coronation—became the site of his rejection by God as king.

10 The word of the Lord came to Samuel: "I regret that I have made Saul
king, for he has turned back from following me and has not performed
my commandments." 11 And Samuel was angry, and he cried to the
Lord all night.

12 And Samuel rose early to meet Saul in the morning. And it was told
Samuel, "Saul came to Carmel, and behold, he set up a monument for
himself and turned and passed on and went down to Gilgal."

13 And Samuel came to Saul, and Saul said to him, "Blessed be you
to the Lord. I have performed the commandment of the Lord." 14 And
Samuel said, "What then is this bleating of the sheep in my ears and
the lowing of the oxen that I hear?"

15 Saul said, "They have brought them from the Amalekites, for the
people spared the best of the sheep and of the oxen to sacrifice to
the Lord your God, and the rest we have devoted to destruction."
(1 Samuel 15:10–15)

15 Why did God regret having made Saul king?

16 What evidences of Saul's pride and hypocrisy do you see in this passage thus far?

17 No matter how much Saul claimed to have fully carried out God's will, there was evidence that he had not. What tactic(s) did Saul use to attempt to explain his actions?

Day 4

You may want to read the rest of 1 Samuel 15. When Samuel delivered his rebuke, Saul tried to "spiritualize" his disobedience. The best of the livestock had been spared so the people could worship God, he suggested (vv. 15, 21). And just in case that wasn't an acceptable reason, Saul implied that it was not his idea but the people's (v. 21).

Later in the conversation, Saul finally admitted that he had done wrong, but he still offered excuses: "I have sinned, for I have transgressed the commandment of the Lord and your words, because I feared the people and obeyed their voice" (1 Samuel 15:24).
First Samuel 15:22–23 reveal the "bottom line" from God's perspective:

> 22 *And Samuel said, "Has the Lord as great delight in burnt offerings and sacrifices,*
> *as in obeying the voice of the Lord?*
> *Behold, to obey is better than sacrifice,*
> *and to listen than the fat of rams.*
> 23 *For rebellion is as the sin of divination [witchcraft,* NKJV*],*
> *and presumption is as iniquity and idolatry.*
> *Because you have rejected the word of the Lord,*
> *he has also rejected you from being king."*

> "Partial obedience, delayed obedience, and surface obedience to impress others are not acceptable to God. He is looking for men and women who will respond with instant, complete, wholehearted, and joyous obedience each time He speaks."
>
> —Del Fehsenfeld Jr.

In summary, consider some things we can learn about obedience from the life of Saul:

- Those who boast about their obedience may be trying to cover up disobedience.
- In God's eyes, nothing is more important than obedience.
- Disobedience reveals a rebellious heart.
- The "smallest" point of disobedience is no small matter. As with witchcraft, rebellion opens us up to the realm and influence of Satan (v. 23a).

It is also important to understand that disobedience brings consequences. Saul lost his position; God took the kingdom from him. Saul had to stand by in shame and watch as someone else accomplished what God had told him to do (v. 28). Saul also lost the godly friendship and counsel of Samuel.

Partial obedience is disobedience. God is not interested in hearing us say, "I'll do anything but ________." Nor are there any acceptable excuses for failing to fully accomplish what He has told us to do.

18 If God were to examine my heart, He would say that:

❍ I am more like Moses—I strive to fully obey God.

❍ I am more like Saul—I often only partially obey God, and then offer excuses or blame others for my disobedience.

❍ I don't really show any concern for whether or not I am obeying Him.

19 According to 1 Samuel 15:22, God takes greater delight when His children obey His voice than in anything else they can bring Him or do for Him. Do you want to please your heavenly Father? If so, write a brief prayer expressing your desire to bring delight to His heart through your obedience.

Day 4

Day 5: Making It Personal

THE OQ (OBEDIENCE QUOTIENT) TEST

What is the single greatest hindrance to revival? Could it be the lack of obedience? Each act of disobedience is a step away from God. Likewise, each act of obedience is a step back toward Him. Remember God's plea in Malachi 3:7: "'Return to Me, and I will return to you,' says the Lord of hosts."

If we were completely honest, many of us would admit that we already know one or more specific steps of obedience we need to take in order to return to the Lord. Perhaps there is something God has told us to do that we've not yet done; something we continue to do that we know is not pleasing to Him; or some limit we have placed on what we're willing to do for Him.

Pause for a moment to pray. Ask God to show you any matters where you are not walking in complete obedience. Ask Him to bring you to a place of willingness and surrender, as you consider the following "obedience quotient" questions.

1. Is there anything I know God wants me to do that I've not yet done? For example,
   - ❍ forgiving someone and being reconciled to him or her?
   - ❍ calling or writing to encourage a Christian brother or sister?
   - ❍ honoring my parents?
   - ❍ devoting more time to my spouse or children?
   - ❍ getting out of debt?
   - ❍ getting rid of some material thing that has captured my heart?
   - ❍ giving something to a person in need?
   - ❍ sharing Christ with a particular person?
   - ❍ showing special honor to the Lord's Day?
   - ❍ developing a daily habit of Bible reading and prayer?
   - ❍ showing hospitality to someone?
   - ❍ surrendering to vocational Christian service?
   - ❍ taking a new job?
   - ❍ quitting a job?
   - ❍ taking care of my body, eating right, and/or exercising?
   - ❍ giving at least 10 percent of my income to the Lord's work?

> "In order to experience revival, most of us do not need to hear more truths; we simply need to obey that which we already know."
>
> Del Fehsenfeld Jr.

This list and those that follow are not intended to be exhaustive. If the thing God has told you to do is not on the list, write it here.

I know God wants me to...

2. Am I continuing to do something that I know God wants me to stop? For example,
   - ❍ a recreational activity or hobby that is consuming too much time?
   - ❍ overspending, failing to pay what I owe?
   - ❍ arguing?
   - ❍ cursing, bad language?
   - ❍ flirting?
   - ❍ gambling?
   - ❍ gossiping, slandering, having a critical spirit?
   - ❍ holding a grudge?
   - ❍ losing my temper?
   - ❍ lying, cheating, stealing from my employer or someone else?
   - ❍ acts of violence?
   - ❍ viewing pornography?
   - ❍ overeating, smoking, drinking, taking drugs, or other addictions?
   - ❍ adultery (emotional or physical)?
   - ❍ too much or the wrong kind of television and movie viewing?

"Obedience to God's Will is the secret of spiritual knowledge and insight. It is not willingness to know, but willingness to DO (obey) God's Will that brings certainty."

—Eric Liddell

If the thing God wants you to stop doing is not on this list, write it below.

I know God wants me to stop...

3. Have I placed any limits on what I am willing to do for God? Am I reluctant to:

   ❍ sacrifice my time in order to serve others?

   ❍ give sacrificially of my possessions and resources to further His kingdom?

   ❍ set aside time on a daily basis for Bible study and prayer?

   ❍ associate with the downcast in order to reach them with God's love?

   ❍ reduce my work hours and, if necessary, my income in order to meet the spiritual needs of my family?

   ❍ move to a new or unfamiliar place in order to be in God's will?

   ❍ break off friendships and relationships that draw me away from Christ?

   ❍ stand alone for righteousness, even at the risk of being misunderstood or ridiculed?

   ❍ make a commitment to be an active part of a local church?

   ❍ [Husbands] love my wife more than I love myself, and provide spiritual leadership for my family?

   ❍ [Wives] respect and submit to my husband?

Record below any additional limitation that you may have placed on pleasing God.

I confess that I have been unwilling to...

"God is God. Because He is God, He is worthy of my trust and obedience. I will find rest nowhere but in His holy will, a will that is unspeakably beyond my largest notions of what He is up to."

—Elisabeth Elliot

4. If you knew that Jesus was going to return three days from now, would you be excited to meet Him because you have been living an obedient life?

   ❍ No. I would be ashamed to meet Christ in my present condition.

   ❍ Yes. I have been living in such a way that I could welcome Christ with gladness.

Day 5

If you answered no, what would you need to do in order to be prepared for His return?

In order to be ready to meet Christ, I would need to...

Determine to begin obeying God immediately—in the "little" and the big things. Remember that, in reality, you may not even have three days—Christ could come at any time! In the meantime, complete, whole-hearted obedience will provide a strong foundation for your life, regardless of what storms may come, and it will prepare the way for the glory of God to be revealed in and through your life.

Seeking Him Together

Opening It Up

1. Last time, we talked about pursuing personal holiness. That's a journey of a lifetime, but it begins with one step and then another. Since the group met last, what blessings or challenges have you experienced in your pursuit of holiness?

Talking It Over

2. Think back to the Faith-Builder story. How would you respond to someone who might have said to this businessman, "What you're doing is not wrong; it's just common business practice—everyone does it! You don't need to confess it or make restitution!"

3. Do you sense that this man obeyed God joyfully or grudgingly? How do you know?

> "I was not born to be free. I was born to adore and to obey."
>
> —C. S. Lewis

4. What does our personal "obedience quotient" reflect about our relationship with God?

Seeking Him Together

5. Read Matthew 7:24–27 aloud. How does obedience to Christ and His Word prepare us to face the inevitable storms of life?

Can you think of a real-life illustration of:

- Someone who built his house (i.e., his life) on the sand and crumbled under pressure? (Be sure not to share unnecessary or private details.)

- Someone who built his house on the rock of obedience to Christ's Word and was sustained through a major storm?

6. What blessings or consequences have you personally reaped from some act of obedience or disobedience in your life?

7. What important lesson did you learn from the account of Moses building the tabernacle (Exodus 39–40)?

8. Why is it so important that we obey God completely? Why is it not enough to obey some, or even most, of what He says?

9. In addition to the four insights listed on page 135 (Day 4), what can we learn about obedience and disobedience from the life of King Saul?

10. If you're comfortable doing so, share a personal testimony of how God has dealt or is dealing with you as a result of the "Making It Personal" exercise. You may want to share a specific step of obedience God led you to take this week.

"Happy is the soul which...holds itself ceaselessly in the hands of its Creator, ready to do everything which he wishes; which never stops saying to itself a hundred times a day, 'Lord, what would you have me to do?'"

—François Fénelon

Praying for Revival

Is there a specific issue of obedience God has been convicting you about, a difficult step of obedience you know you need to take, or a particular area where you chronically find it difficult to obey God? Pair up with one other person and share your answer to that question. Be as honest as possible—remember, you can't obey God without His grace, and God gives grace to those who humble themselves! Spend a few moments praying for each other regarding what has been shared. Offer to contact your prayer partner during the coming week to see how he or she is doing.

Lesson 8

Clear Conscience:

Dealing with Offenses toward Others

The first seven lessons in this study have focused primarily on the vertical aspect of revival—that is, our relationship with God. Now we turn the corner to consider the horizontal implications of revival—that is, how a right relationship with God affects our relationships with others.

The apostle Paul understood the necessity of both dimensions. He said, "I always take pains to have a clear conscience toward both God and man" (Acts 24:16). The King James Version translates this verse: "And herein do I exercise myself, to have always a conscience void of offence toward God, and toward men." Paul was intentional about being right at all times with God and with others. As far as it was in his power, he wanted to be sure there was no offense standing between him and any other person.

The commitment to have a clear conscience is an important key to personal and corporate revival. When our conscience is clear, we have nothing to be ashamed of. In this lesson we will explore what it means to have a clear conscience toward others and discover some practical steps to obtaining and maintaining a clear conscience.

MEMORY VERSE

"Herein do I exercise myself, to have always a conscience void of offence toward God, and toward men."
(Acts 24:16 KJV)

Going Deeper in the Word

Romans 2:12–16
Hebrews 9:11–14
1 Peter 3:13–17
1 John 3:19–24

Day 1: Faith-Builder Story

1 Can you think of a time when the Holy Spirit convicted you of a sin you had committed against someone, and you had no peace in your conscience until you made it right with that person? If so, write about your experience.

Read the following story about a man who was willing to do whatever it took to have a clear conscience with God and his employer.

> I was an engineering supervisor with one of the largest defense contractors for the U.S. government; in that role, I had top-level security clearance. During a revival crusade at my church, God began to convict me about being dishonest years earlier when I had filled out the security clearance forms. Specifically, I had lied about my use of drugs while I was a college student. The form made it clear that any willful false statement could result in "imprisonment of up to ten years and a fine of up to $10,000." I had used drugs repeatedly while I was in college and on a few isolated occasions after that. I knew that if I told the truth on the application, I probably wouldn't get the job. So I lied.
>
> I remember lying awake at night; I just couldn't get the whole thing out of my mind. At first, I tried to "appease" God by taking care of some smaller things in my life. But even after I got those right, I still had no peace. Finally, I told my wife that if I was going to be right with God, I had to resubmit my paperwork. I explained to her that this could lead to a full FBI investigation and that I might lose my job.
>
> I amended my paperwork, with an attached note explaining that I had given my life to Jesus Christ, and felt I needed to confess that I had lied when I originally filled out my security forms. I asked them to forgive me and told them how sorry I was that I had lied. I can still remember walking down the hall with that envelope in my hand. Satan kept harassing me and telling me that I was blowing my job and life for nothing.
>
> It was almost a week before I heard anything. Finally, my boss called me into his office. The director of security was there. "The navy has asked

"Satan kept harassing me and telling me that I was blowing my job and life for nothing."

that you be suspended pending an investigation," he said. "I will need to take your security badge."

I was allowed to continue working and even to supervise my crew, but I no longer had security clearance into the building. I was given a desk in the hallway—and consequently found myself having constant opportunities to explain what God had done in my life! People told me I was crazy to trust the security department to handle my case. But I told them that the security department was not who I was trusting—I was trusting God.

I continued as the supervisor on the project for the next several months. Finally I was required to undergo a full Department of Defense investigation. My boss became fearful that the investigation might drag on indefinitely. I felt torn between Christ and the world. How could I have expected them to understand? Finally I was told that the FBI had cleared me. I completed that assignment and later was reassigned to another area that provided an even better situation for my family and me.

"The utter helplessness of being dependent on God alone was exactly what I needed."

I have never regretted what I did. The utter helplessness of being dependent on God alone was exactly what I needed.

2 If this man had come to you seeking counsel as to whether or not he should admit his deception to his employer, what advice would you have given him? (Be more specific than "You should/should not admit it.")

Before we can have a conscience "void of offense" toward others, our conscience must first be clear with God. Hebrews 10:19–23 explains the only way that is possible:

Day 1

[19] Therefore, brothers, since we have confidence to enter the holy places by the blood of Jesus, [20] by the new and living way that he opened for us through the curtain, that is, through his flesh,... [22] Let us draw near with a true heart in full assurance of faith, with our hearts sprinkled clean from an evil conscience and our bodies washed with pure water. [23] Let us hold fast the confession of our hope without wavering, for he who promised is faithful.

3 Why can we draw near to God with a clean conscience and full assurance? Take time now to thank God for His provision that makes it possible for us to approach Him with a heart that is pure and a conscience that is clear.

Day 1

Day 2: Truth Encounter

WHAT DOES IT MEAN TO HAVE A CLEAR CONSCIENCE?

Having a clear conscience means there is no obstruction in our fellowship with God or anyone else. It means we are careful to avoid sinning against God or others with our words, actions, or attitudes. It also means that when we do sin, we quickly repent, admit our failure to all offended parties, ask their forgiveness, and make whatever restitution is necessary.

To have a clear conscience toward others means we have taken whatever steps are necessary to deal with every sin we may have committed against every other person. It means we can look everyone we know in the eyes without shame and know that we are right with them, insofar as it depends on us.

The Old Testament prophet Samuel was a hero in Israel. He had been a faithful spiritual counselor for many years. His life was stable and his leadership had always been reliable, even during times of national chaos. In 1 Samuel 12 we find that the entire nation has gathered to listen to Samuel. He is now an old man and his reputation is well known among all the people. He asks the people an astonishing question and receives an equally remarkable response.

> [1] *And Samuel said to all Israel, "Behold, I have obeyed your voice in all that you have said to me and have made a king over you.* [2] *And now, behold, the king walks before you, and I am old and gray; and behold, my sons are with you. I have walked before you from my youth until this day.*
>
> [3] ***"Here I am; testify against me before the Lord and before his anointed. Whose ox have I taken? Or whose donkey have I taken? Or whom have I defrauded? Whom have I oppressed? Or from whose hand have I taken a bribe to blind my eyes with it? Testify against me and I will restore it to you."***
>
> [4] *They said, "You have not defrauded us or oppressed us or taken anything from any man's hand."* (1 Samuel 12:1–4; emphasis added)

Key Point 

To have a clear conscience means to have no unconfessed sin between you and God or any other person.

Insight 

Often considered the last of the judges and the first of the prophets, Samuel was called by God when just a child (1 Samuel 3). He provided leadership and stability in Israel for many years and lived long enough to anoint both Saul and David as kings. He died around 1000 BC.

Day 2

4 Think about how Samuel might have worded his speech if he had been speaking to a modern-day audience. Paraphrase in your own words the portion that is in boldface above, as if it were being spoken in the context of a family gathering, a workplace, or a church.

5 Why do you think Samuel could be so vulnerable and transparent with the people he led?

6 The people of Israel knew Samuel well—they had observed his life for many years. What does their response tell us about Samuel's character?

Insight

Like Samuel, we should be able to stand before everyone we know and have no one accuse us of doing wrong to them and failing to make it right.

Samuel's life beautifully illustrates what it means to have a clear conscience. He could stand before these people who knew him and had observed his life, ask them what wrong he had done to any of them, and have not one accuser. Not one!

Day 2

7 If you were to stand before every person you know and ask the questions that Samuel asked of those who knew him best, would you get the same response?

- ❍ Yes, the response would be the same. To the best of my knowledge, my conscience is fully clear and I would have no accusers.
- ❍ No, I would receive a different response. Some could justifiably accuse me of wronging them and of never having sought to make it right.

Any child of God who is serious about seeking the Lord and experiencing personal revival must be committed to maintain a clear conscience toward others. This is where the rubber meets the road—this is the context in which genuine repentance, humility, and holiness are demonstrated practically.

This week we are dealing with one of the most powerful and practical principles of personal revival. It can also be one of the most difficult. If you desire to obey God by obtaining and maintaining a clear conscience, take a moment to pray this prayer from your heart, and then seal your commitment to the Lord by signing your name below:

> *Lord, I want to have a conscience that is clear toward every person I know. Please reveal to me any issues I need to resolve with others and, by Your grace, I will do whatever You show me I need to do to make these matters right.*
>
> *Signed* ______________________________

Day 3: **Truth Encounter**

RECONCILED WITH GOD AND OTHERS

Have you ever considered that Jesus takes personally what we do or say to another person? Two New Testament passages make this particularly clear. In Matthew 25, Jesus commends the righteous for ministering to His practical and personal needs and condemns the wicked for failing to do so. Both groups are perplexed as to when or how they might have done this.

> **Insight**
>
> In Matthew 25:31–46 Jesus is speaking of a judgment that will take place during His earthly reign, described in Revelation 20:4–6.

> *37 Then the righteous will answer him, saying, "Lord, when did we see*
> *you hungry and feed you, or thirsty and give you drink? 38 And when did*
> *we see you a stranger and welcome you, or naked and clothe you?*
> *39 And when did we see you sick or in prison and visit you?"*
>
> *40 And the King will answer them, "Truly, I say to you,* ***as you did it to***
> ***one of the least of these my brothers, you did it to me....*** *45 As you*
> *did not do it to one of the least of these, you did not do it to me."*
> (Matthew 25:37–40, 45; emphasis added)

Acts 9 is the familiar account of the conversion of Saul of Tarsus. Read the opening portion below:

> *1 But Saul, still breathing threats and murder against the disciples of the*
> *Lord, went to the high priest 2 and asked him for letters to the syna-*
> *gogues at Damascus, so that if he found any belonging to the Way,*
> *men or women, he might bring them bound to Jerusalem.*
>
> *3 Now as he went on his way, he approached Damascus, and suddenly*
> *a light from heaven flashed around him. 4 And falling to the ground he*
> *heard a voice saying to him, "Saul, Saul, why are you persecuting me?"*
> *5 And he said, "Who are you, Lord?" And he said, "I am Jesus, whom*
> *you are persecuting."* (Acts 9:1–5)

8 According to verses 1 and 2, who was Saul persecuting?

9 When Jesus spoke to Saul, who did He say Saul was persecuting (vv. 4–5)?

10 What insight do you see in these two passages (Matthew 25 and Acts 9) about how God views our actions toward other people?

The good and the evil that we do to others, we do to Jesus. This truth alone should provide reason enough for us to always strive to maintain a clear conscience. Would you lie to Jesus? Would you steal from Him? Would you believe unfounded rumors about Him, then spread them as truth? Would you get angry at Christ? Would you belittle or criticize Him? Would you hold a grudge against Him or give Him the silent treatment? Jesus says, *"As you did it to one of the least of these my brothers, you did it to me"* (v. 40; italics added).

11 Ask God to bring to mind anyone(s) that you may have treated in a way that was harmful to them (and therefore to Christ). Seek His forgiveness for your sin against Him and against the other individual(s) and ask God to show you how to gain a clear conscience with that person.

Revival and reconciliation are inseparable. *You cannot be right with God, and not be right with your fellow man.* When our relationship with God is revived, our relationships with others are impacted. Broken relationships are mended; bitterness, grudges, critical spirits, anger, and conflict are replaced by genuine love, forgiveness, humility, and oneness.

Key Point !

Revival and reconciliation go hand in hand.

Consider the revival that swept much of Canada and portions of the United States in the early 1970s. The epicenter of this movement was Ebenezer Baptist Church of Saskatoon, Saskatchewan. During the initial days of this revival, two brothers were marvelously reconciled. Prior to that, they had not spoken to one another for two years, even though they attended the same church! However, one evening God broke through their hardness and pride, and they fell into each other's arms, sobbing. The church could not help but notice the drastic change in them, and God greatly used their testimony to spread and deepen the work of revival.

Right relationships—especially within the family of God—are one of the most powerful means of communicating the gospel to a lost world. Our God is a reconciling God, and when believers cannot get along with each other or fail to resolve conflicts biblically, we actually discredit the gospel. When God's people are reconciled to each other, we demonstrate the power of the gospel and make it believable.

In Ephesians 2, Paul explains that because Christ has reconciled us to God, we can now be reconciled to others.

Insight

In Ephesians 2, Paul is referring specifically to the reconciliation of Jews and Gentiles to God and to each other. However, the principle applies to other relationships as well.

> [12] *Remember that you were at that time separated from Christ, alienated from the commonwealth of Israel and strangers to the covenants of promise, having no hope and without God in the world.*
>
> [13] *But now in Christ Jesus you who once were far off have been brought near by the blood of Christ.* [14] *For he himself is our peace, who has made us both one and has broken down in his flesh the dividing wall of hostility* [15] *by abolishing the law of commandments and ordinances, that he might create in himself one new man in place of the two, so making peace,* [16] *and might reconcile us both to God in one body through the cross, thereby killing the hostility.* (Ephesians 2:12–16)

12 On what basis can sinners who are alienated from God be reconciled to Him (v. 13)?

13 On what basis can people who are alienated from each other be reconciled to each other (vv. 14–16)?

Day 3

Through the cross of Christ, those who were once separated from God can draw near to Him. And through that same cross the "dividing wall of hostility" that exists between us and others has been broken down, making it possible for us to be reconciled and to live at peace with each other.

14 Pause for a moment and take a quick personal inventory. Do you have a broken or strained relationship with any other person?

❍ Yes

❍ Not that I am aware of

15 Check any of the following attitudes, responses, or issues that are currently in your heart:

❍ hurt feelings

❍ critical spirit

❍ desire for revenge

❍ anger

❍ a grudge

❍ unresolved conflict

❍ bitterness

❍ keeping score

❍ other: __________

16 Read Matthew 5:23–24. With this Scripture in mind, reflect on the various ways that you are currently serving God (for example, teaching a class, giving, attending worship services, witnessing). Now visualize a traffic signal hanging between you and that activity. Is God calling you to "stop" or to continue? Is He "giving you the green light" because your conscience is clear, or has He turned the light red, indicating that you need to be reconciled with someone before your worship and service can be acceptable to Him?

Day 3

Day 4: **Making It Personal**

Reconciliation sounds wonderful, doesn't it? Who wouldn't want to experience the thrill of having a long-lost friend restored or of turning an enemy into an ally? But these things do not just happen. At least one party must take the pathway of humility and accept personal responsibility for any wrong attitudes or actions. (In the next lesson, we'll consider the role of forgiveness in reconciliation.)

! Key Point

If we have wronged another, we must humble ourselves and do whatever is required to gain a clear conscience with God and that person.

Reconciliation requires that we take whatever steps are necessary to obtain a clear conscience toward those we have offended or wronged in any way. As we read in Day 4, Jesus emphasized this process in His Sermon on the Mount:

> [23] *So if you are offering your gift at the altar and there remember that your brother has something against you,* [24] *leave your gift there before the altar and go. First be reconciled to your brother, and then come and offer your gift.* (Matthew 5:23–24)

17 Why is reconciliation with others more important to God than whatever gifts we may offer to Him? How are our relationships with God and others interconnected?

Jesus said that if we recall that another believer has something against us, we must stop what we're doing and deal with it immediately—even if we're in the middle of a worship service! We are not to proceed any further in our effort to worship, serve, or give an offering to Him. We must first go and be reconciled to that offended brother. Until we do, all attempted spiritual activity will be meaningless.

So how do you go about getting a clear conscience? Here are some practical guidelines to help you get started. We'll look at the first two steps today, and then cover several others on Day 5.

1. Make a list.

Set aside some quality time when you can be alone and uninterrupted. Begin with prayer. Purpose to agree with God about whatever He shows you. *Then, ask God to search your heart and to remind you of each person you have wronged or with whom you have an unresolved conflict.*

Make a list of each person God brings to mind. As you write each name, also write down how you have sinned against that person. Be as specific as possible about the ways you have wronged that individual.

Here are some questions to jump-start your thinking. These questions are not intended to be comprehensive—God may point out other areas or categories of people with whom you need to clear your conscience. Some of the issues God brings to mind may be in your past—others may be current. Whether your offense took place fifty years ago or fifty minutes ago, if you have not dealt with it, put it on the list.

Use the following questions to help you determine:

With whom do I need to clear my conscience? Whom have I sinned against and never gone back to seek their forgiveness and make it right?

A. Is your conscience clear with your family?

- Have you broken any promises to your family? Have you broken your marriage vows?
- Are you deceiving your family in any way?
- Are you slothful or negligent in your duties at home?
- Do you have any habits that irritate or frustrate your family?
- Are you angry, resentful, or abusive toward any family member?
- Have you wounded the spirit of your mate?
- Have you withheld love from your mate or any of your children?
- Have you dishonored your parents or your mate's parents?
- Have your failed to provide for your family, or to give yourself to your mate sexually?

Insight 

If your first thought when you think of someone is anger, resentment, dread, or fear, chances are that person needs to be added to your list!

Day 4

B. Is your conscience clear with your church family?

- Have you been guilty of gossip, slander, or a critical spirit toward your pastor or any of the leaders of your church?
- Has God placed any area of service on your heart that you have been unwilling to perform?
- Do you have critical thoughts and attitudes toward anyone in your church? Have you verbalized those thoughts to others?
- Do you portray a "better-than-thou" attitude to your church family?
- Have you failed to give at least a tithe of your income back to the Lord?
- Have you failed to follow the Lord in believer's baptism?
- Have you abused your role of leadership in the church in any way?
- Have you been a hypocrite—serving in the church, leaving an impression of being spiritual, while covering up disobedience or lack of a heart for God?

"There is no pillow so soft as a clear conscience."
—French Proverb

C. Is your conscience clear with the lost world?

- Have you stirred up or contributed to any disputes in your neighborhood or community?
- Have you stolen from any place of business (shoplifting, were undercharged and didn't call attention to it, etc.)?
- Do you obey traffic laws, building codes, and other local ordinances?
- Is your name well spoken of by your neighbors and the vendors with whom you conduct business?
- Would the people in your community conclude that you are a Christian by observing your lifestyle?
- Have you cheated on your income taxes? On exams or papers at school?

D. Is your conscience clear in your workplace?

- Have you spoken disrespectfully to or about your supervisors?
- Do you have any unresolved disputes with fellow workers?
- When you do have a disagreement at work, do you seek to resolve it quickly and biblically, or do you display anger and bring others in on it needlessly?

- Do you work faithfully and diligently? Are you always honest about why you are taking time off?
- Do you abuse company policies?
- Have you stolen any items or money from your employer or cheated on expense reports?

E. Is your conscience clear from your past?

- Do you have any unresolved conflicts with family members? church members, leaders, staff? neighbors? supervisors, fellow workers? classmates, teachers, professors?
- Have you committed any crime that you have never confessed to the proper authorities?
- Have you lied to anyone about anything in an attempt to avoid consequences for some wrong you have done?

Is there anything else of which God is convicting you that needs to be made right? Any sin—past or present—that you have never cleared up with the person affected by it? Any person you couldn't look in the eye with a clear conscience? Add each person and offense God brings to mind to the list of those you need to clear your conscience with.

2. Seek God's forgiveness.

Every sin against another person is first a sin against God (2 Samuel 12:13). Pray through the list you have made and seek God's forgiveness for how you have sinned against Him by wronging others.

"The testimony of a good conscience is the glory of a good man: have a good conscience and thou shalt ever have gladness."

—Thomas à Kempis

Once you have made your list and sought God's forgiveness, you are ready to begin clearing your conscience with the individuals on your list. If you're feeling overwhelmed with the length of your list, remember that God will never ask you to do anything that He will not give you the grace—the desire and power—to do. And remember that *God gives grace to the humble.* As you humble yourself and begin to clear your conscience, He will walk each step of the way with you, however hard the process may be and however long it may take.

Day 5: **Making It Personal**

The steps you take in today's session may be some of the most challenging and difficult ones you have ever taken in your spiritual journey. But with every step of humility, you will receive more of God's grace and will be one step closer to experiencing the blessing of a conscience that is "void of offence toward God, and toward men" (Acts 24:16, KJV). As you work through your list, you will discover that there is no joy or freedom like the joy and freedom of having a clear conscience with God and every person.

Unlike the other "Making It Personal" exercises in this study guide, you will not be asked to record your responses on paper today. Instead, you will be encouraged to actually begin the process of obtaining a clear conscience—whatever that means and whatever it takes. This is one time when it is especially important to be a "doer" and not just a "hearer" of the Word! Don't let the Enemy steal from you the freedom of a clear conscience. Take those first steps—today!

Now that you've made a list of people with whom you need to clear your conscience, here are some further guidelines.

3. Purpose to seek forgiveness from every person you have wronged.

Listing names does not clear your conscience; it only gives you a map. Until you actually go and confess your wrongdoing and seek forgiveness, your conscience will not be clear. Ideally, go and speak to each individual face-to-face. If that is not possible, talk to them on the telephone. Writing a letter is generally not wise, as it is more difficult to communicate your heart and to sense the response of the person whose forgiveness you are seeking.

Ask the Lord to give you wisdom in the timing of when to approach the people on your list, especially when you are dealing with a sensitive issue. Also, you may need to seek counsel from a pastor or mature, godly friend, as to how to best deal with some particularly difficult or complex situations.

Write a brief prayer expressing your commitment to obtain a clear conscience with every person on your list, and asking the Lord for grace to follow through on your commitment.

If the other person was also at fault, leave it to the Holy Spirit to convict him or her. God is asking you to clear *your* conscience, not theirs!

4. Choose your words carefully.

Be humble. Don't offer excuses or make accusations, regardless of how wrong the other person may have been. Humble yourself and confess your sin. When he returned home, the prodigal son said to his father, "I have sinned against heaven and against you" (Luke 15:18). Be specific about how you have sinned against that person. Don't just apologize or say, "I'm sorry"—if you want forgiveness, ask for it.

5. Where necessary, make restitution.

If you have cheated or stolen from someone, offer to restore what you have taken. (See the Faith-Builder story in Lesson 7, about the furniture manufacturer who made restitution for stealing designs from other companies.)

6. Pursue reconciliation of the relationship.

To whatever extent it is possible and appropriate, the goal is restoration of the relationship that has been damaged or lost. (In some cases, such as those involving immorality, physical or sexual abuse, or illegal activities, it may not be appropriate to restore the relationship.) Once you have confessed your wrongdoing and sought forgiveness, you can then begin the process of rebuilding the broken relationship.

"I have to make an effort to keep my conscience so sensitive that I can live without any offense toward anyone."

—Oswald Chambers

7. Face the hardest situations first.

You may be tempted to put off going to certain people on your list. Perhaps the situation is extremely hard for either or both of you to face. Nevertheless, do the hard things first. If you don't, you may never go. If you do, the others will come easier because you will have lost much of your sense of fear and dread.

8. Don't stop until you have finished.

The process of clearing your conscience may take months or even years, but don't quit! God has called you to do this, and He will see you through. If there is someone on your list that you don't know how to find, ask God to bring them across your path and commit to Him that the first chance He gives you, you will clear your conscience with that person. You may be amazed at what God does—He is more concerned with this matter than you are; watch for His hand in assisting you. Enjoy the journey and the fruit of obedience.

9. Determine to maintain a clear conscience.

Take time regularly to let God search your heart and show you any way you have sinned against Him or others. Seek to keep short accounts—to deal with each offense as God convicts you of it.

On the next page you will find several additional guidelines to keep in mind as you seek to obtain and maintain a clear conscience.

Additional Guidelines for Clearing Conscience

! Key Point

When trying to clear your conscience, match the scope of your confession to the scope of the offense.

Scope of Confession

When you set out to clear your conscience, remember that the scope of your confession should be as large—and only as large—as the scope of your sin. In other words, we need to admit our wrong and seek the forgiveness of all those who have been affected by our wrongdoing. Here are some guidelines to help you determine the appropriate scope for your confession.

- *Private confession.* Sin committed against God needs to be confessed to God.
- *Personal confession.* Wrongs done to another individual need to be confessed to God and to that person—for example, lying, stealing, anger, slander, immorality.
- *Public confession.* If our sin was against a group of people or has become common knowledge, we need to seek forgiveness from all those who have been affected. Examples include public outbursts of anger, an adulterous relationship that is public knowledge and has tarnished the testimony of Christ, hypocritical lifestyles, stealing from church funds, etc.

! Key Point

Situations involving confession of moral failure need to be handled with special prayer, wisdom, and godly counsel.

Cautions Regarding Confession of Moral Sin

- When sexual sin has been broadly known and needs to be confessed publicly, use discretion and avoid sharing unnecessary details. In most cases, it would be wise to limit the scope of confession to God, then to spouses (if applicable), and possibly to church leaders (for accountability and discipline). However, if the offender is in a position of spiritual leadership, the scope of confession may need to be greater (see 1 Timothy 5:20).
- If a man has been guilty of lusting after a woman in his heart, he should *not* confess that sin to the woman (though he may need to seek her forgiveness for such offenses as not treating her in a virtuous way, etc.). He should confess his sin of lust privately to God and consider sharing his struggle with one or a few godly brothers in Christ (without naming the woman).
- If a husband or wife needs to clear their conscience with his or her mate in relation to marital infidelity, it is generally best to seek counsel from a mature spiritual leader and to have a godly third party available to walk through the process with the couple.

Day5

Seeking Him Together

Opening It Up

1. What insight(s) in this week's lesson were either new to you or were something you already knew but needed to be reminded of?

Talking It Out

2. The man in the Faith-Builder story cleared his conscience, and it became quite public. Though he would not have chosen for it to happen that way, how might that exposure have proven to be a blessing and benefit to this man in his spiritual growth?

3. How would you define what it means to have a clear conscience? Why is this such an important concept for believers to understand and practice?

4. How did the prophet Samuel illustrate what it means to live with a clear conscience?

Seeking Him **Together**

5. Discuss this statement from Day 3: "Revival and reconciliation are inseparable. *You cannot be right with God, and not be right with your fellow man."* Why do you think there is such a strong connection between our relationship with God (the vertical) and our relationships with others (horizontal)?

6. Discuss the "scope of confession." If someone's sin affects a group of people, or becomes known publicly, how should that person go about clearing his conscience?

7. Why is it so important to obtain and maintain a clear conscience with our families and in our churches? What are the blessings of doing so and the possible consequences of not doing so?

8. Dream a little. If every believer in your community purposed to have a clear conscience and to pursue reconciliation of broken relationships, how might the impact be seen and felt? How might people's view of Christians and Christianity be affected?

9. If you feel the freedom to do so, share an example of how you have already begun to apply this lesson. Have you gone to someone you had wronged and sought forgiveness? What happened?

As always, when sharing how God is working in your life, be careful not to reflect negatively on others or reveal specific details that should not be known publicly.

Praying for Revival

Pair off with someone you feel comfortable opening up to about spiritual needs. Take a few minutes to relate how God is dealing with you in relation to clearing your conscience. Is there someone you know you need to go to—an offense you need to confess, a relationship you need to reconcile—but are struggling to do so? Pray for each other and offer to hold each other accountable to follow through on whatever direction God has given.

Lesson 9

Forgiveness:

Setting Your Captives Free

Forgiveness. The gift everyone wants to receive but finds hard to give. It's not easy to forgive. Yet forgiveness is one of the most important elements of personal and corporate revival. "Who is a God like you, pardoning iniquity?" the Old Testament prophet asked (Micah 7:18). When we repent of our sins, God mercifully releases us from our debt, through the great cost of His Son's death on the cross. As recipients of His forgiveness, we are called to forgive those who sin against us. When we release our offenders through forgiveness, we discover the key that unlocks the prison doors of our own hearts and sets us free to experience greater peace and joy than we ever dreamed possible.

"Be kind to one another, tenderhearted, forgiving one another, as God in Christ forgave you."
(Ephesians 4:32)

Luke 17:1–4; 23:32–47
Ephesians 4:29–5:2

Day 1: **Faith-Builder Story**

1 In your experience, have you found it easy or hard to forgive others? Why?

Read the following testimony of one woman's struggle to forgive. Then answer the questions.

> My husband and I had looked forward to the revival meetings at our church with much anticipation and expectation. We felt there were many people in our church who desperately needed revival and renewal. Little did we know what God had in store for our lives.
>
> One unforgettable night during the revival, in the presence of a godly counselor, my husband confessed to me that he had been involved in homosexual relationships before we were married, and that he had continued one of those relationships until recently.
>
> As you can imagine, for the next several weeks I lived on an emotional roller coaster. At times I felt a sense of exhilaration that my husband had been freed from a secret he had kept buried all those years. Then, moments later, I would feel overwhelmed by a sense of betrayal, hurt, and anger. The one constant was an unexplainable confidence that God was in control, and I held to the promise that He would never forsake me. The Bible came alive to me for the first time in years, and I found assurance and peace through His Word. I realized my loneliness could be replaced with the strong love of the Lord, a love that I could always trust.
>
> I remember telling the Lord that I accepted the circumstances He had given me, even if I were never to understand all the "whys." Thus began the healing process and the ability to forgive. The dictionary definition of *forgiveness* is "to cease to feel resentment against; pardon; to give up claim to requital; to grant relief from payment." This was a pretty big request. How could I forgive someone who had hurt me beyond anything I could ever imagine, who had taken away the deep trust I had in him, and who had destroyed the purity of our relationship? I learned that forgiveness was not something I could do on my own, but that Christ could forgive through me.

"The one constant was an unexplainable confidence that God was in control, and I held to the promise that He would never forsake me."

"I learned that forgiveness was not something I could do on my own, but that Christ could forgive through me."

Forgiveness came when I realized who I was apart from Christ. God revealed many things to me about my own life that were just as sinful (in His eyes) as what my husband had done. I realized that God takes all sin seriously and that for me to judge one sin to be greater than another was . . . well, I was playing God. God is not partial, and He hated my sin just as much as He hated my husband's sin. I am a sinner saved by grace, nothing more. If I truly accepted who Christ is, then I had the ability to forgive.

We sought Christian counseling to help us work through some of our difficulties, and over time, we began communicating on a level of love and unselfishness. The months that followed were not easy, but they began to bring us closer than we had ever been before. We agreed to hold each other accountable, and through that accountability developed a new sense of trust. Miraculously, God began bringing people into our lives who were struggling with similar problems, and we have had the privilege of seeing other marriages and relationships healed.

I would be wrong in leading you to believe it's all been wonderful since those first few months. Occasionally I still struggle with mistrust, unforgiveness, anger, and a sense of betrayal. There have been moments when I wished that he had never told me. But I wouldn't trade any of the pain for the freedom my husband gained from his confession and for the victory he experienced over his sexual addiction. I wouldn't trade any of the pain for the times we've been able to share our experience with others in order to help their relationships. And I wouldn't trade any of the pain for the life-changing opportunity I have been given to walk the pathway of forgiveness.

"I wouldn't trade any of the pain for the renewed relationship I have with my Lord, my husband, and our children."

2 What insights about the character and ways of God helped this woman to forgive her husband?

Day 1

3 Take time to pray the Lord's Prayer below. Meditate on the connection between forgiving others and experiencing God's forgiveness for your sins:

> 9 *Our Father in heaven,*
> *hallowed be your name.*
> 10 *Your kingdom come,*
> *your will be done,*
> *on earth as it is in heaven.*
> 11 *Give us this day our daily bread,*
> 12 *and forgive us our debts,*
> *as we also have forgiven our debtors.*
> 13 *And lead us not into temptation,*
> *but deliver us from evil.* (Matthew 6:9–13)

Day 2: Truth Encounter

THE SEVENTY-TIMES-SEVEN VIRTUE

In your opinion, which of the following statements is true?

❍ If I am careful, I can go through life without ever being hurt.

❍ I will get hurt only if I am mean or unkind to others.

❍ Even if I try hard to avoid it, I will be hurt at some time in my life.

The fact is, somewhere, sometime, somebody will treat us wrongly. That is an unavoidable reality of life. So how should we respond to those who hurt us, especially if they do so intentionally? We may wonder with the apostle Peter, "Lord, how often will my brother sin against me, and I forgive him? As many as seven times?" (Matthew 18:21).

Humanly speaking, it was admirable that Peter was willing to forgive the same person seven times! But the kind of forgiveness Jesus advocated was (and is) supernatural. Imagine Peter's astonishment when Jesus replied, "I do not say to you seven times, but *seventy times seven*" (v. 22).

Jesus' command is staggering. We must be willing to forgive the same person time after time after time. Forgiveness unlimited!

Jesus continued His response to Peter's question, using a parable to explain the necessity and nature of true forgiveness.

> *23 Therefore the kingdom of heaven may be compared to a king who
> wished to settle accounts with his servants. 24 When he began to settle,
> one was brought to him who owed him ten thousand talents. 25 And
> since he could not pay, his master ordered him to be sold, with his wife
> and children and all that he had, and payment to be made.*
>
> *26 So the servant fell on his knees, imploring him, "Have patience with
> me, and I will pay you everything." 27 And out of pity for him, the master
> of that servant released him and forgave him the debt. 28 But when that
> same servant went out, he found one of his fellow servants who owed
> him a hundred denarii, and seizing him, he began to choke him, saying, "Pay what you owe." 29 So his fellow servant fell down and pleaded
> with him, "Have patience with me, and I will pay you." 30 He refused and
> went and put him in prison until he should pay the debt.*
>
> *31 When his fellow servants saw what had taken place, they were greatly distressed, and they went and reported to their master all that had taken place.*
>
> *32 Then his master summoned him and said to him, "You wicked*

Key Point 

We cannot avoid being hurt and wronged by others. Therefore, we cannot avoid the need to forgive others.

Insight 

A *talent* was a Jewish measurement of weight approximately equal to the full weight a man could carry. In Jesus' day, ten thousand talents of silver would have been worth the equivalent of many millions of dollars. The *denarius*—a silver Roman coin commonly in circulation in Israel—was the usual daily wage for a manual laborer. A hundred *denarii*, therefore, were worth a tiny fraction of what ten thousand *talents* were worth.

servant! I forgave you all that debt because you pleaded with me. [33]*And should not you have had mercy on your fellow servant, as I had mercy on you?'* [34] *And in anger his master delivered him to the jailers, until he should pay all his debt.*

[35] *So also my heavenly Father will do to every one of you, if you do not forgive your brother from your heart.* (Matthew 18:23–35)

4. How much money did the servant owe his master? What was the likelihood of the servant's ever paying off this kind of debt?

5. What motivated the master's forgiving response?

6. The servant's massive debt had been canceled. What possible reason did he have to be so ruthless and cruel in trying to collect from his fellow servant?

7. In your own words, summarize the message Jesus was trying to communicate in this parable.

8 Can you think of an instance in which you treated someone who had wronged you similar to the way this forgiven servant treated his debtor?

The vital message of the parable is found in the master's question, "Should you not have had mercy on your fellow servant, as I had mercy on you?" (v. 33). In other words, the forgiven must be forgiving.

Key Point !
As forgiven people, we must be willing to forgive others.

In this parable each child of God is reminded of the following:

- We once carried a debt of sin far beyond any hope of our ever meeting its payment.
- God justly could have sold us into eternal slavery and anguish.
- God freely gave us full pardon, sacrificing His own "resources" (His Son) in order to pay our debt.
- Having been shown such mercy, we should be ever merciful to others.

9 Write a brief prayer expressing to the Lord your personal response to this account in Matthew 18.

Day 3: Truth Encounter

PROVIDENTIAL PURPOSES

Insight

Joseph, the older son of Jacob's wife Rachel, probably born around 1746 BC, led an up-and-down life. Honored by his father; sold into slavery by his brothers. Given a responsible position by Potiphar; unjustly thrown into prison. As second in command to Pharaoh, he could have taken revenge against his brothers. But he had learned to see God's hand in *all* phases of his life, and chose to forgive.

Jesus taught that we are to forgive without limit. Let's look at an example of forgiveness in action. You are probably familiar with the story of Joseph and the abuse he received at the hands of his brothers. Because they were jealous, Joseph's brothers sold him into slavery, then lied to their father by saying that he had been killed by a wild beast. (You can read the story in Genesis 37.)

Meanwhile, Joseph found himself in Egypt, where he distinguished himself as a faithful man. He soon became a trusted servant in the household of an important government official, but his employer's wife falsely accused him and he was cast into prison. Even then, however, Joseph refused to be overcome by adverse circumstances, and he found favor with the jailer. Although he used his God-given wisdom to minister to some of his fellow inmates, Joseph was forgotten and remained in prison for another two years.

Finally, Joseph's day of freedom came. Pharaoh, the king of Egypt, had a dream, and only Joseph could interpret its meaning. As a result, Joseph was catapulted from prisoner to "vice pharaoh" in one day.

In his new position Joseph had the authority to punish those who had treated him unjustly. But observe his actions when he confronted his brothers who had come to Egypt for food. (They did not recognize him at first; they knew only that this powerful man held their lives in his hands.)

Key Point

God is sovereign over the hurts others inflict on us and will use them for redemptive purposes, if we let Him.

> *4 So Joseph said to his brothers, "Come near to me, please." And they*
> *came near. And he said, "I am your brother, Joseph, whom you sold*
> *into Egypt. 5 And now do not be distressed or angry with yourselves*
> *because you sold me here, for God sent me before you to preserve life.*
> *6 For the famine has been in the land these two years, and there are yet*
> *five years in which there will be neither plowing nor harvest. 7 And God*
> *sent me before you to preserve for you a remnant on earth, and to keep*
> *alive for you many survivors.*
>
> *8 "So it was not you who sent me here, but God. He has made me a*
> *father to Pharaoh, and lord of all his house and ruler over all the land of*
> *Egypt."* (Genesis 45:4–8)

Years later, when his brothers expressed fear that Joseph would take vengeance on them after the death of their father, Joseph once again expressed faith in the sovereign control and purposes of God:

> [19] *But Joseph said to them, "Do not fear, for am I in the place of God?*
> [20] *As for you, you meant evil against me, but God meant it for good, to*
> *bring it about that many people should be kept alive, as they are today.*
> [21] *So do not fear; I will provide for you and your little ones." Thus he*
> *comforted them and spoke kindly to them.* (Genesis 50:19–21)

10 Try to put yourself in Joseph's shoes. What would have been a natural, human response to his circumstances?

11 How did Joseph's view of God and His purposes affect his perspective on his trials and his response to his brothers?

Notice that Joseph was not looking for someone to blame, nor was he seeking revenge. Even though wrongs had been done, Joseph knew God had been in control of his life all along. Joseph was able to see the hand of God in times of adversity as well as in times of prosperity. He realized that the purposes of God were of much greater importance than his personal comfort. Therefore, he was able to forgive and bless those who mistreated him.

12 Think about a situation where someone has wronged or hurt you deeply. In light of what you have seen in the story of Joseph and his response to his brothers, write a brief paragraph expressing faith in God's sovereign purposes for you in your situation. If you have already seen (at least in part) how God has taken what others meant for evil and used it for good, record that as well.

Tip +

Later in the New Testament, the apostle Paul affirmed the same providential care in Romans 8:28: "And we know that for those who love God all things work together for good, for those who are called according to his purpose."

Day 4: **Making It Personal**

> **+ Tip**
> The "Making It Personal" section in this lesson is longer than usual. You may want to allow extra time or even take an additional day to complete this exercise.

Every child of God who wants to experience personal revival must be willing to deal honestly and fully with any unforgiveness that may be in his or her heart. Today's study is designed to help you face some of the barriers that could keep you from choosing the pathway of forgiveness.[1]

Have you ever found yourself making (or thinking) any of the following statements? As you work through this section, pay special attention to any of these perspectives that reflect the way you think or feel. Then consider how God may want to adjust your thinking as it relates to the issue of forgiveness.

1. "There's no unforgiveness in my heart."

It is possible to live with the seeds of unforgiveness for so long that we become blinded to its presence in our life. The following questions will help open your eyes to any unforgiveness that may have become lodged in your heart.

a. Have you ever been hurt? Put a check next to any of the following hurts you have experienced:

- ❍ lied to
- ❍ promise(s) broken
- ❍ neglected by grown children
- ❍ violent crime against self or a loved one
- ❍ treated unfairly by an employer
- ❍ parents divorced
- ❍ slandered/falsely accused
- ❍ divorced by mate
- ❍ mate committed adultery or other sexual sin
- ❍ rejected by parents
- ❍ stolen from
- ❍ cheated in a business/financial deal
- ❍ rebellious/wayward son or daughter
- ❍ belittled
- ❍ alcoholic parent or mate
- ❍ abandoned by parent or mate

❍ publicly humiliated

❍ abused (physically, emotionally, sexually)

❍ other ______________________

b. As you reflect on the ways you have been wronged, do you find any of these statements to be true?

❍ Every time I think of [person or offense], I still feel angry.

❍ I have a subtle, secret desire to see [person] pay for what he/she did to me.

❍ Deep in my heart, I wouldn't mind if something bad happened to [the person(s)] who hurt me.

❍ I sometimes find myself telling others how [person] hurt me.

❍ If [person's] name comes up, I am more likely to say something negative about him/her than something positive.

❍ I cannot thank God for [person].

These statements are an indication that we have not fully forgiven all those who have sinned against us.

God's Word says that if we say we have not sinned, even though His Spirit shows us otherwise, we deceive ourselves and the truth is not in us (1 John 1:8). Have you deceived yourself into believing that you have forgiven everyone who has sinned against you? As God examines your heart, does He find any unforgiveness there?

c. Put a check in this box if you would agree with God that there is unforgiveness in your heart. ❍

2. "There's no way I could ever forgive [person] for [*offense*]. He (she) hurt me too deeply."

a. What are some of the hurts Jesus suffered from us?

Isaiah 53:3–7 ______________________________

Psalm 22:6–7, 16 ______________________________

Key Point !

Forgiveness means that I fully release the offender from his debt. It means fully cleaning his record. It is a promise never to bring up the offense against him again (to God, to others, or to the offender himself).

Day 4

"To be a Christian means to forgive the inexcusable, because God has forgiven the inexcusable in you. This is hard; . . . how can we do it? Only, I think, by remembering where we stand, by meaning our words when we say in our prayers each night, 'Forgive us our trespasses as we forgive those who trespass against us.' We are offered forgiveness on no other terms. To refuse it means to refuse God's mercy for ourselves."

—C. S. Lewis

b. **How has God dealt with us who have sinned against Him so greatly?**

Ephesians 2:4–5 ________

Isaiah 43:25; Hebrews 10:17 ________

Micah 7:18–19 ________

c. **How does the New Testament command us to respond to those who wrong us?**

Luke 6:27 ________

Luke 17:3–4 ________

Romans 12:17–21 ________

d. **According to Colossians 3:13, what should be the measure—the standard—of our forgiveness?**

e. On that basis, what offense is "too great" to forgive?

f. **Would God command us to do something that He would not enable us to do?**

Day 4

g. How are we enabled to forgive (see Philippians 2:13)?

"Forgiveness is the fragrance the violet sheds on the heel that has crushed it."

—Mark Twain

3. "They don't deserve to be forgiven."

a. What did we do to earn or deserve God's forgiveness?

Romans 5:8

Ephesians 2:4–9

b. What are the reasons we should extend forgiveness to those who sin against us?

❍ The offender is genuinely sorry for what he has done.

❍ We have been forgiven an infinite debt by God, so we forgive as we have been forgiven.

❍ God commands us to forgive.

❍ The offender promises never to do it again.

❍ The offense was an "understandable mistake."

4. "If I forgive them, they're off the hook!"

We may feel that if we forgive another, justice will not be served—they'll get off scot-free. The problem is, we have put *ourselves* in the position of a "bill collector."

What does Romans 12:19 have to say about "bill collecting"?

Letting the offender off *your* hook does not mean they are off God's hook. Forgiveness involves transferring the prisoner over to the One who is able and responsible for meting out justice. It relieves us of the burden and responsibility to hold them in prison ourselves.

Here's something to think about: Would I be willing for God to deal with me in the same way that I want to see my offender dealt with?

5. "I've forgiven them, but I'll never be able to forget what they did to me."

a. According to these Scriptures, when God forgives us, what does He promise to do?

Jeremiah 31:34; Hebrews 10:17 __________

Psalm 103:12 __________

! Key Point

Forgiveness is not forgetting. It is a transaction in which I release my debtor from the obligation to repay his debt.

An omniscient God cannot *forget*. But He does promise not to "remember our sins" or hold them against us. God does not ask us to *forget* the wrong that has been done to us, but simply to *forgive*. However, the attitude of our heart, when we think of the offense, can be an indicator of whether or not we have truly forgiven.

b. When you think of the person who has hurt you most deeply, which of the following attitudes do you experience?

- ❍ emotional churning
- ❍ sense of rest and relinquishment
- ❍ desire for revenge
- ❍ desire to see him spiritually restored
- ❍ hard to ask God to bless him
- ❍ desire for God to bless him
- ❍ hard to see his good qualities
- ❍ gratefulness to God for this person
- ❍ want others to know what he did
- ❍ humbled by how greatly you have sinned against God and how much He has forgiven you

+ Tip

If you are uncertain about how to handle a particular section biblically, seek counsel from a godly third party. Some situations may require legal intervention or church discipline. In some cases, such as those involving sexual abuse or immorality, reconciliation on the horizontal level may not be appropriate.

6. "I believe I have forgiven, but I still struggle with feelings of hurt."

a. According to the following passages, what must we be willing to do in addition to forgiving those who sin against us?

Luke 6:27–31 __________

Romans 12:17–21 __________

Day 4

The act of forgiveness is only the starting place for dealing with those who wrong us. The initial act of releasing the offender must be followed by a commitment to invest positively in his or her life. This investment is the key to experiencing emotional healing and wholeness. In situations where it is not possible or appropriate to rebuild the relationship with an individual, we can still invest in their lives through prayer.

b. What are some practical ways you could "return good for evil" or invest in the life of someone who has wronged you?

Tip 

Whenever possible, we should seek to rebuild the relationship between ourselves and the offender.

7. "I won't forgive!"

Ultimately, forgiveness comes down to a choice. It is a choice that God both commands and enables. But some simply refuse to make that choice.

a. According to the following Scriptures, what can we expect if we refuse to forgive those who sin against us?

Matthew 6:14–15
Matthew 18:32–35
2 Corinthians 2:10–11

b. What are some of the physical, emotional, and spiritual "tormentors" (Matthew 18:34 KJV) we might experience in our lives if we are unwilling to forgive?

"Bitterness robs us of joy and peace. It hijacks us, taking us places we never wanted to go, doing things we never wanted to do, and making us people we never wanted to be."

—Bill Elliff

Day 4

c. From the list above in question b, circle those consequences of unforgiveness that you have personally experienced at one time or another.

Choosing the pathway of forgiveness can be extremely difficult. You may have been sinned against in ways that have caused enormous pain and consequences in your life. Just working through this lesson may be opening up some wounds or memories you'd just as soon not face. Be assured that if you are willing to walk into the pain, God will go there with you. Hard as it may be to forgive those who have sinned against you, you will experience great freedom as you choose to obey God, by His grace.

Day 4

Day 5: Making It Personal

Has God revealed any lack of forgiveness in your heart? Do you desire to be set free from the prison of unforgiveness? Are you ready to choose the pathway of forgiveness? If so, here are some steps that will help you deal with the hurts and offenses you have experienced.

1. Make a list of the people who have wronged you. Next to each name, write the offense(s) that person has committed against you. Then record how you have responded to their wrongdoing. Be as honest and specific as possible—have you loved them, prayed for them, forgiven them? Or have you resented them, withheld love from them, slandered them to others, been bitter toward them?

Person	Their Offense	My Response

2. Thank God for each person who has wounded you, for they are His instruments to sanctify you—to mold and conform you to the image of Jesus.

3. Confess to God, and then to the offender, any wrong responses you may have had (unforgiveness, hatred, bitterness, gossip). Be careful not to blame them for your wrong attitudes or responses. Remember that God does not hold us responsible for the wrongs others have done to us; He only holds us responsible for how we respond to what others do to us.

4. As Christ has forgiven you, fully forgive each offender. Remember that forgiveness is not a feeling; rather, it is a choice and an act of the will. It is a commitment to clear the other person's record and never to hold that offense against him again.

Keep in mind that emotional healing may involve a process, but actual forgiveness can be extended in a moment. Don't wait to forgive until you feel emotionally healed from the wound; instead, choose to forgive and let God begin the process of true healing in your life.

Tip 

You may want to use a separate piece of paper for this exercise, or photocopy this page to record your answers more privately.

"To forgive is to set the prisoner free, and then discover the prisoner was you."

—Author Unknown

Day 5

Verbalize to the Lord your forgiveness of each of the individuals listed under 1, above. *"Father, as you have forgiven me, so I choose to forgive* [person] *for* [name the offense]."

> "Forgiveness ought to be like a cancelled note—torn in two and burned up, so that it never can be shown against one."
>
> —A. W. Tozer

5. Build bridges of love. Ask God to show you how you can "return good for evil" (Luke 6:27–31; Romans 12:17–21). List some practical ways you can invest positively in the lives of those who have wronged you.

6. "Comfort him" and "reaffirm your love for him" (2 Corinthians 2:7–8). If the offender is repentant, assure him of God's forgiveness and your love, so he will not be "overwhelmed by excessive sorrow" (v. 7) and so Satan will not be allowed to take "advantage" of you through any unforgiveness (v. 11, NKJV).

[1] These statements and steps toward forgiveness in Days 4 and 5 of Lesson 9 have been adapted from "Freedom Through Forgiveness" by Nancy Leigh DeMoss, ©2001, published by Life Action Ministries.

Seeking Him Together

Opening It Up

1. Share an example of how you have experienced God's grace and forgiveness in a fresh way since beginning this study.

> "To be forgiven is such sweetness that honey is tasteless in comparison with it. But yet there is one thing sweeter still, and that is to forgive."
>
> —C. H. Spurgeon

Talking It Over

2. In the Faith-Builder story, the wife said, "I learned that forgiveness was not something I could do on my own, but that Christ could forgive through me." How could that insight be helpful to someone struggling to forgive another?

3. Why do you think people were drawn to this couple to seek out their help, even though they may not have known what the couple had been through?

> "I say to the glory of God and in utter humility that whenever I see myself before God and realize even something of what my blessed Lord has done for me, I am ready to forgive anybody anything."
>
> —Martyn Lloyd-Jones

4. It is easier to forgive others when we consider the magnitude of the forgiveness we have received from God. Share a brief testimony about how God has forgiven you. (This could be a salvation testimony or a witness of how God restored you after you had strayed from Him.)

Seeking Him **Together**

5. Ephesians 4:32 says, "Be kind to one another, tenderhearted, forgiving one another, as God in Christ forgave you." How would you describe the way God has forgiven us? (Consider Psalm 103:10–12, for starters.) How should His forgiveness affect the way we deal with those who sin against us?

Caution

Be careful to not violate any confidence by sharing details that shouldn't be made public.

6. Think about a time when someone forgave you, or you forgave someone else. How did giving or receiving forgiveness benefit your life?

7. What are some of the consequences of refusing to forgive? What kind of toll have you seen bitterness take, either in your life or in others you know?

8. Of all the qualities that should distinguish Christians from the world, why is forgiveness so significant? What effect might the act of our forgiving someone have on an unbeliever who watches our actions?

9. Do any of the seven statements in Day 4 describe your attitude (for example, "There's no unforgiveness in my heart")? Which one(s)?

10. Have you walked through the process this week of forgiving one person or more? If you feel the freedom to do so, share what God is doing in your life as you have been choosing the pathway of forgiveness.

Praying for Revival

Pair off with another group member with whom you can share your heart openly. Briefly discuss how God is dealing with you in relation to forgiveness. Discuss the following questions:

- Is there anyone you have not fully forgiven in your heart?
- What steps do you need to take to obey God and forgive those who hurt you?

Discuss with your partner any other specific ways God has been dealing with you through this lesson. Pray for each other regarding the needs you have shared. Ask God to give each person in your group the grace to fully forgive others as He has forgiven you.

Optional 

Have an impromptu "praise session." As a group, decide on a way that you want to praise the Lord for His amazing forgiveness. This could be a time of sentence prayers, or you could choose a chorus to sing. Be as simple or as creative as you wish. Use this praise time to reinforce in your own mind the reason and motivation you have to forgive others.

Sexual Purity:

The Joy of Moral Freedom

Just watch five minutes of television ads or page through a magazine, and you'll notice that Western culture is saturated with sexual images and is intent on promoting the "joys" of so-called sexual freedom. God created us as sexual beings, and our sexual drive is a good and powerful part of us. But when those desires surpass our desire for God, or when we seek to fulfill them apart from God's prescribed means and timing, they can be our downfall.

The Bible's perspective on sexual purity has gotten a bad rap as repressive, outdated, legalistic, and no fun. Nothing could be further from the truth. Staying sexually pure, or committing to moral purity, can be a big step toward personal revival, deep joy, and true freedom.

"For this is the will of God, your sanctification: that you abstain from sexual immorality."
(1 Thessalonians 4:3)

Genesis 39:2–12
Psalm 119:1–16
Proverbs 5
1 Corinthians 6:12–20

Day 1: Faith-Builder Story

1 How important do you think a believer's sexual life is in his or her walk with God? Explain.

Read the following story of how God rescued a home ravaged by immorality. Then answer the questions.

> "Pete had been sitting on a powder keg for years. Turmoil made the powder keg explode."

Pete had always thought he was an open guy—he could tell anyone anything about himself. Except for one thing. He had never confided in a single person about his struggle with pornography and sexual lust. No one knew. Even after he met and married Sue, the problem lingered. For a while he would "behave," but sooner or later his wandering thoughts would entice him to buy a magazine or to watch a movie. Eventually his toying with immorality took him where he never thought he would go—into two extramarital affairs, both with women in the church where he held a leadership position.

Sue could tell something wasn't right. Pete was acting strangely; even his appearance seemed harder. But whenever she questioned him, he assured her that everything was fine. Sue grew more confused, frustrated, and angry. They began having horrible arguments. If Pete was telling the truth, why was she so suspicious of him? Maybe she really was going insane. The strife in their home became so oppressive that their two children began having nightmares.

By keeping his involvement with pornography and the affairs secret, Pete had been sitting on a powder keg for years. Finally, the turmoil at home made the powder keg explode. Sue asked Pete to leave and go stay with some friends from church. Unknowingly, Sue was sending Pete to stay in the home of the woman with whom he was having an affair!

Things began to unravel in Pete's secret world when his church held a two-week revival crusade. Pete was worried and guilt-ridden. He doubted that he could attend these services without coming clean about the sinful way he was living. Finally, one night after a crusade service, Pete could stand the conviction no longer. He confessed to Sue that he had been unfaithful to her. Sue was shocked. She had somehow

believed Pete's assurances that he was not sexually involved with another woman. She ran into the church sanctuary and literally fell on the altar, sobbing. "It was a feeling worse than hearing that a family member had died," Sue later explained. She went home and began to pack.

Sometime during the course of the long evening and night, God pierced through the intensity of Sue's emotions and convinced her of one thing, one crucial thing: it was time to forgive! Sue did not receive this very openly at first; she argued with God most of the night. But when the Holy Spirit reminded her that it was from the cross—from the intense agony of the cross—that Jesus spoke and gave forgiveness, Sue knew He wanted her to do the same. In the midst of her pain—not after it eased a little, but while it hurt deeply—God was compelling her to grant forgiveness. By the next morning, God had prepared her to call Pete.

"I believe that at that moment I could have become a very bitter old woman —at age thirty! But God protected me from that."

"At that moment," Sue recalls, "I too was at a crossroad in life. But when I spoke the words of forgiveness to Pete, all the anger and confusion that had been bottled up inside me for months was released. I believe that at that moment I could have become a very bitter old woman–at age thirty! But God protected me from that."

The following evening, while the revival crusade was still in progress, Pete stood before the church and confessed, resigning his ministry position. For nearly two years he had planned what he would do if he ever got caught; now none of those plans seemed proper. He wanted only to be clean before God—a decision he had reached even before Sue called to forgive him.

With the help of family, friends, and their church—which set up a restoration team—Pete and Sue began the long, hard process of rebuilding their marriage. Since that time they have counseled with many couples whose homes have been ravaged by some form of immorality.

2 Who was affected by Pete's moral sin, and how?

Day 1

3 What factors contributed to Pete's bondage to immorality? What factors contributed to his being set free?

The psalmist prayed, "How can [one] keep his way pure? By guarding it according to your word. With my whole heart I seek you; let me not wander from your commandments!" (Psalm 119:9–10). The Word of God provides the resources for any child of God to walk in purity in every area of his life.

4 If you share the psalmist's desire to seek God and obey His commands, write a prayer asking God to guard your heart and make and keep you morally pure.

Day 1

Day 2: Truth Encounter

CALLED TO SEXUAL PURITY

Battling lust is not a twenty-first century phenomenon; God's people have always had to deal with sexual temptation. The apostle Paul confronted this matter head-on when he wrote the church in Thessalonica about their Christian conduct:

> [1] *Finally, then, brothers, we ask and urge you in the Lord Jesus, that as you received from us how you ought to live and to please God, just as you are doing, that you do so more and more.*
>
> [2] *For you know what instructions we gave you through the Lord Jesus.*
> [3] *For this is the will of God, your sanctification:* ***that you abstain from***
> ***sexual immorality;*** [4] *that each one of you* **know how to control his**
> **own body in holiness** *and honor,* [5] *not in the passion of lust like the*
> *Gentiles who do not know God;* [6] *that* **no one transgress and wrong**
> **his brother in this matter,** *because the Lord is an avenger in all these things, as we told you beforehand and solemnly warned you.*
>
> [7] *For God has not called us for impurity, but in holiness.* [8] *Therefore*
> *whoever disregards this, disregards not man but God, who gives his Holy Spirit to you.* (1 Thessalonians 4:1–8; emphasis added)

Insight 

Thessalonica, where Paul founded a flourishing church in AD 49 or 50, was the capital of the Roman province of Macedonia. Roman morality tended to be lax in sexual matters, and the worship of some Roman deities involved ritual prostitution. Paul had to underscore for the new believers in Thessalonica that Christian faith meant (among other things) the restriction of sex to marriage.

5 According to these verses, what are some important reasons to live a life that is morally pure?

(v. 1) It p________ God.

(v. 3) Under divine inspiration, the biblical authors instructed us to a__________ from sexual immorality.

(v. 3) It is the w________ of God that we be holy in every area, including sexually.

(v. 5) We k________ God.

(v. 6) Other believers are our b__________ in Christ. We are family!

(v. 6) The Lord will a__________ all those who wrong others sexually.

(v. 6) The Scripture solemnly w__________ us against sexual sin.

(v. 7) God has c____________ us to holiness.

(v. 8) God has given His H________ S__________ to live in us.

Day 2

Regardless of how spiritual we may claim (or pretend) to be, the truth is that we are no more spiritual than our sexual conduct and thought life. In this passage Paul gives three specific exhortations regarding our sexual behavior.

a. Have absolutely nothing to do with any form of immorality. (*"Abstain from sexual immorality"* v. 3.) Instead, we should determine to be morally blameless in all our thoughts, activities, and relationships. In his letter to the Ephesians, Paul makes this point even more explicitly:

> [3] *Among you there must not be even a hint of sexual immorality, or of any kind of impurity, or of greed, because these are improper for God's holy people.* [4] *Nor should there be obscenity, foolish talk or coarse joking, which are out of place, but rather thanksgiving.* (Ephesians 5:3–4)

"A little lust is not okay. That's why God calls us to the daunting standard of *not even a hint.* This means there's no place for lust to exist peacefully in our lives. We're to fight it on every front."

—Joshua Harris

6 What do you think Paul is including when he says that we should abstain from all sexual immorality? How much impure behavior or talk is acceptable for a believer? Why are these things "out of place" for Christians?

7 What are some forms of immorality that many professing believers today would tolerate, excuse, or even condone?

b. Be a student of your own person. (*"That each one of you know how to control his own body in holiness and honor, not in the passion of lust"* vv. 4–5.) Know what entices you to immorality and avoid it. Know what encourages you to be pure and activate it.

8 What do you think it means to control your body in holiness and honor, rather than in the passion of lust?

9 How well do you know yourself? List any specific places, people, situations, and activities you need to *avoid* because they could make you more vulnerable to sexual temptation.

10 What are some relationships and activities that are *helpful* to you in your pursuit of purity?

c. Be sure you do not take advantage of or wrong others sexually. (*"That no man transgress and defraud his brother in this matter"* v. 6 [NASB]; *"that in this matter no one should wrong his brother or take advantage of him"* [NIV].) Rather, seek to live a life that edifies and encourages others to be morally pure.

11 Why do you think God considers it such a serious offense to sin morally against another believer? What are some ways we can exercise caution and avoid wronging others morally?

"In 1 Thessalonians 4:6 (NASB), the word rendered transgress means 'to sin against,' which includes the concept of stepping over the line and exceeding the lawful limits.... Defraud means to selfishly, greedily take something for personal gain and pleasure at someone else's expense.... Whenever believers seek to satisfy their physical desires and gain sexual pleasure at the expense of another, they have violated this command."

—John MacArthur

Day 2

Day 3: **Truth Encounter**

PROVERBS AND PURITY

! Key Point

Sexual sin is a serious obstacle to spiritual well-being.

"If we would rehearse in advance the devastating consequences of immorality, we would be far less prone to commit it."

—Randy Alcorn

12 Below is a list of some *positive* motivations to be morally pure. Check the ones that are (or should be) important to you.

- ❍ To keep my family together
- ❍ To maintain a good name/reputation
- ❍ To set an example for others who are younger
- ❍ To set a good example for those who are new in their faith
- ❍ To provide a Christ-honoring testimony to those who are lost
- ❍ To keep my job
- ❍ To reduce the risk of getting certain diseases
- ❍ To honor my spouse
- ❍ To keep myself pure for my marriage partner
- ❍ To strengthen the cause of Christ and His kingdom
- ❍ To avoid hypocrisy
- ❍ To keep myself from greater vulnerability to other temptations and sin
- ❍ Because God commands it
- ❍ Because I love God
- ❍ Because I love my spouse
- ❍ Because I love my children
- ❍ Because I don't want to ruin someone else's life
- ❍ Because I don't want to destroy another family
- ❍ So I can sleep at night
- ❍ So I don't have to live in fear of getting caught
- ❍ So my life can be a usable instrument for God's purposes

13 How many potential *negative* consequences of sexual sin can you think of?

Clearly, when one is thinking righteously, rationally, and responsibly, a life of moral purity is the only wise and proper choice. But life isn't always rational, and human nature isn't always responsible. The onslaught of moral temptation can be almost overwhelming, even for believers. In the face of such a severe and constant assault on our souls, we must actively guard ourselves against moral failure.

In unmistakably clear language God's Word deals with immorality's characteristics, causes, consequences, and solutions. The book of Proverbs speaks at length to the subject of moral purity. Take a brief look at some of these passages below.

14 Proverbs talks about the adulteress, whose words, attitudes, dress, and behavior entice men to be immoral. Read Proverbs 7:1–27. What are some of the characteristics of an immoral woman?

15 How does the foolish man respond to the immoral woman (7:22–23)? What causes him to respond this way (see Proverbs 5:12–13)?

"I must choose between sexual fantasies and intimacy with God. I cannot have both. When I see that God offers me joys and pleasures that sexual fantasies don't, this is a breakthrough. But that breakthrough will come only when I pursue God, making Him the object of my quest—and when I realize that fantasies are only a cheap God-substitute. Running to them is running from God."

—Randy Alcorn

16 What are the consequences of yielding to the sensual woman (6:27–29; 7:26–27)?

17 How does the wise man respond to the sensual woman (4:23, 25–27; 5:7–8)?

18 How can a believer protect himself/herself from moral impurity (4:20–27; 5:15, 17–18; 6:23–24)?

Day 4: Making It Personal

"All right," you may be saying, "I'm convinced. Immorality is a grave danger, and I need to aggressively guard my heart against it. But how?" To get you started, here are some practical safeguards for moral purity gleaned from God's Word. There are six safeguards in today's study and another six in Day 5. Each safeguard includes some *Heartcheck* questions and reflections to help you apply that particular point. [1]

As you prayerfully read through these biblical principles for sexual purity, agree to cooperate with God and commit yourself to the pathway of moral purity—for a lifetime.

Insight

Every Christian needs to be intentional about safeguarding his/her heart and mind against immorality.

1. Recognize your potential for moral failure.

Therefore let anyone who thinks that he stands take heed lest he fall. (1 Corinthians 10:12)

All of us are vulnerable to the lust of the flesh and the lust of the eyes. History is filled with examples of men and women who fell prey to sexual temptation even though they had previously walked in intimacy with God. The most committed of believers are susceptible if they relax their guard or believe they are above being tempted.

Heartcheck: Acknowledge to the Lord that apart from Him you could be vulnerable to any kind of sin, and that you need His protection in every area of your life, including your sexual life.

2. Realize that you don't have to give in.

No temptation has overtaken you that is not common to man. God is faithful, and he will not let you be tempted beyond your ability, but with the temptation he will also provide the way of escape, that you may be able to endure it. (1 Corinthians 10:13)

As a child of God, you have His divine grace available to you at all times. You do not have to be overcome; you can overcome. The choice is yours. (If we are honest, many would have to admit that we often fall because inwardly we *want* to sin.)

Heartcheck: Thank the Lord for His promise to provide a way of escape from every temptation. Agree with Him that there is no temptation you cannot overcome by His grace.

"Who shall ascend to the hill of the Lord? And who shall stand in his holy place? He who has clean hands and a pure heart." (Psalm 24:3–4)

3. Resolve to be pure.

> *Therefore, preparing your minds for action, and being sober-minded, set your hope fully on the grace that will be brought to you at the revelation of Jesus Christ. As obedient children, do not be conformed to the passions of your former ignorance, but as he who called you is holy, you also be holy in all your conduct.* (1 Peter 1:13–15)

Battles can be won or lost before the enemy is ever engaged. Don't wait until you are face-to-face with sexual temptation before you decide how you will respond. *That's too late!* Go on the offensive—before the temptation comes—by resolving in your heart to be morally pure, by God's grace.

Heartcheck: Have you purposed to be pure, no matter what or how strong the temptation? Make a commitment to God that, whatever it takes, you will make moral choices that are pleasing to Him.

4. Remove all bitterness.

> *See to it that no one fails to obtain the grace of God; that no "root of bitterness" springs up and causes trouble, and by it many become defiled; that no one is sexually immoral or unholy like Esau, who sold his birthright for a single meal.* (Hebrews 12:15–16)

The hurts of the past and our refusal to forgive those who have wronged us provide fertile ground for bitterness to flourish. Bitterness, left unchecked, makes us more apt to succumb to—or even pursue—sensuality and to subconsciously justify it in our mind, on the basis of how deeply we have been hurt. Bitterness is like poison; it defiles.

Forgiveness is the only antidote. You cannot hold on to harbored hurts and pursue purity at the same time.

Heartcheck: Ask God to show you if there is any "root of bitterness" in your heart. If there is, release it to God, and receive His grace to forgive the offender and to help you deal with the hurt he/she has caused.

"In times when I'm tempted, I'll say to myself, 'Don't pack a lunch for lust!' I must not pamper or provide even a little snack for the lust of my heart to feed on."

—Joshua Harris

5. Restrain your fleshly desires.

Put on the Lord Jesus Christ, and make no provision for the flesh, to gratify its desires. (Romans 13:14)

You cannot indulge your flesh in one area and expect to conquer it in another. Do not allow even one area of compromise. Giving in on one issue (no matter how small) weakens your resistance and will make you more vulnerable to sin in other matters that may have even greater consequences.

Heartcheck: Is there any area in which you are indulging sinful, fleshly desires (e.g., in relation to food, spending habits, your tongue, etc.)? How can you "put on the Lord Jesus Christ" instead of gratifying your flesh in that area?

6. Reject anything that could lead you into moral bondage.

And I have seen among the simple, I have perceived among the youths, a young man lacking sense, passing along the street near her corner, taking the road to her house in the twilight, in the evening, at the time of night and darkness. (Proverbs 7:7–9)

By walking toward and hanging out near the house of a seductive woman, under cover of darkness, the young man in this proverb put himself in a situation where his natural response would be to sin. He set himself up for moral failure.

We cannot live in a cave, but we can exercise some control over what we encounter during the routine of our lives. Little choices may seem insignificant or justifiable. But if those choices could lead us into temptation, they need to be avoided at all costs.

> *Heartcheck:* Are there any items or influences in your home, your car, or your workplace that could lure you to be morally impure? Determine to get rid of them without delay. Make a list of places and people that could entice you into immorality, and resolve to avoid them.

Write a prayer expressing your response to what God has said to your heart as you have meditated on these first six safeguards for moral purity.

Day 5: Making It Personal

Today we will look at six more insights that will help safeguard our sexual purity. Take time to briefly review the list from Day 4. Then prayerfully seek God's help in coming to an honest estimate of where you stand in developing a life of moral purity that will bring Him honor.

7. Run from every form of evil.

> *So flee youthful passions and pursue righteousness, faith, love, and peace, along with those who call on the Lord from a pure heart.* (2 Timothy 2:22)

If you find yourself in a potentially compromising situation, flee! Do not linger to consider your options. Don't rely on your reason or willpower. Rely on God; He has already told you what to do: run!

> *Heartcheck:* Are you currently involved in any activity, situation, or relationship that (a) is immoral, or (b) could lead you to moral compromise? What does God want you to do about it? Write out your answer. (Use another piece of paper or some sort of "code," if you are concerned about your response being seen.) Do whatever you know God wants you to do.

"Keep as far as you can from those temptations that feed and strengthen the sins which you would overcome. Lay siege to your sins, and starve them out, by keeping away the food and fuel which is their maintenance and life."

—Richard Baxter

8. Renew your mind with the Word of God.

> *Finally, brothers, whatever is true, whatever is honorable, whatever is just, whatever is pure, whatever is lovely, whatever is commendable, if there is any excellence, if there is anything worthy of praise, think about these things.* (Philippians 4:8)

Wrong actions stem from wrong thoughts. If we are to change our behavior, we must first change how we think. God's Word has the power to reform our habits by cleansing our thoughts and renewing our minds (Romans 12:1–2). But we must assume our responsibility to engraft God's Word into our hearts by reading, memorizing, and meditating on it.

Day 5

Heartcheck: What are you doing to fill your mind and your heart with the pure Word and ways of God? Is that sufficient? Are you allowing any ungodly influences to shape your thinking (books, magazines, music, movies)? What change(s), if any, do you need to make?

9. Recruit help.

> *Confess your sins to one another and pray for one another, that you may be healed. The prayer of a righteous person has great power as it is working.* (James 5:16)

It is extremely difficult to achieve victory in any struggle with sin, especially of a moral nature, without the help of godly friends. If you find yourself failing morally (or enslaved to any other sinful habit), identify a mature, godly believer (of the same sex) and humble yourself by admitting your need to that person. Ask him or her to pray for you and to hold you accountable in whatever specific areas you need help.

"I know of no sin that will do more to deaden a man's spiritual vitality than the sin of moral impurity."

—Del Fehsenfeld Jr.

Heartcheck: Who knows your innermost personal struggles and is committed to pray for you and to join you in believing God for freedom and victory? Are you being honest with that person and making yourself accountable on a regular basis? If you do not have someone involved in your life in that way, ask God to show you who you can approach and ask for help.

10. Remember the consequences.

> *But each person is tempted when he is lured and enticed by his own desire. Then desire when it has conceived gives birth to sin, and sin when it is fully grown brings forth death.* (James 1:14–15)

In the heat of temptation, sin is tantalizing. Afterward, it is completely destructive. Think ahead to the anguish you could bring on yourself and your loved ones if you choose to yield to immorality.

Heartcheck: Make a list of several painful consequences that could result from your giving in to moral sin. Transfer that list to a small card or piece of paper. Put it somewhere where you will be reminded to review it regularly.

11. Refuse to remain in defeat and depression.

The righteous falls seven times and rises again. (Proverbs 24:16a)

Have you failed morally? God cannot bless the sin of your past. But He can—and He will—bless a broken and a repentant heart. There is no sexual sin too great for God to forgive. He will not restore your virginity if you have given that away; but He will restore your purity. Do not allow your defeats to keep you defeated; allow His mercy to keep you humble and reliant upon His grace. You can experience victory, in spite of momentary or even major setbacks.

Heartcheck: Thank God that through the power and cross of Christ, you do not have to live under the domination of sin but have been set free to obey and follow Him.

12. Rely on the Holy Spirit.

But I say, walk by the Spirit, and you will not gratify the desires of the flesh. (Galatians 5:16)

I just can't do it. I can't stay pure! you may be thinking. You're right. You can't…not on your own. But you can live a pure life—inside and out—as you rely on the indwelling Spirit of Christ. The Lord Jesus lived a blameless and pure life even while wearing the robes of humanity. The very power that raised Jesus from the dead is able to "keep you from stumbling, and to present you blameless before the presence of his glory with great joy" (Jude 24).

Heartcheck: Write a prayer expressing your desire to be filled with the Holy Spirit and to yield to Him in every area of your life, rather than fulfilling the natural desires of your flesh.

Tip

You may want to use a separate piece of paper for this exercise, or photocopy this page to record your answers more privately.

To review, and as an aid in memorizing the twelve safeguards for moral purity, match each one to its proper description below.

___ 1. Recognize your potential for moral failure.

___ 2. Realize that you don't have to give in.

___ 3. Resolve to be pure.

___ 4. Remove all bitterness.

___ 5. Restrain your fleshly desires.

___ 6. Reject anything that could lead you back into bondage.

___ 7. Run from every form of evil.

___ 8. Renew your mind with the Word of God.

___ 9. Recruit help.

___10. Remember the consequences.

___11. Refuse to remain in defeat and depression.

___12. Rely on the Holy Spirit.

A. I may need to avoid certain places or people in order to stay out of temptation's way.

B. I can't be pure on my own. I need God.

C. I cannot indulge my flesh in one area and expect to conquer it in another.

D. If I have fallen, God wants to forgive and restore me.

E. Forgiving past hurts increases my resistance to sexual temptation.

F. I need to keep in mind just how destructive sin can be.

G. I need to determine to obey God before I'm faced with temptation.

H. The prayers and accountability of others can help me in this battle.

I. God's grace is available to grant me victory over moral sin.

J. I need to engraft God's Word into my thought life.

K. I, like every believer, am vulnerable to the lust of the flesh and the lust of the eyes.

L. If I find myself in a potentially compromising situation, I need to flee!

Thus far we've dealt with some pretty heavy issues—forgiving those who've hurt us, maintaining sexual purity, and so on. You may be wondering how you can experience consistent victory in such difficult areas. But there's a secret that makes it all possible: *Christ living in us!* Lesson 11 will be a great encouragement to you; don't miss it.

---

[1] The list of twelve safeguards for purity in Days 4 and 5 of Lesson 10 originally appeared in "Sensuality: Winning the War Against the Flesh" by Del Fehsenfeld Jr., *Spirit of Revival* magazine, July 1986, vol. 14, no. 2, pp. 12–13, published by Life Action Ministries.

Seeking Him Together

Opening It Up

1. Think back to the lesson on forgiveness; have you taken a concrete step toward forgiving someone? If so, and if it's the kind of thing you can tell without violating a confidence, share with the group how God has been setting you free through forgiveness.

2. Why do you think it is valuable to include a lesson on moral purity in a study on personal revival?

"There is dullness, monotony, sheer boredom in all of life when virginity and purity are no longer protected and prized. By trying to grab fulfillment everywhere, we find it nowhere."

—Elisabeth Elliot

Talking It Over

3. Review the Faith-Builder story. How can moral unfaithfulness of any kind (sexual, emotional, fantasizing, etc.) damage a marriage?

4. What safeguards could a couple put in place to help avoid infidelity?

5. Why do you think sexual sin of all types has become so prevalent among professing believers today?

6. If you were giving advice to a teenage son or daughter about why and how to keep morally pure, what are some things you would say?

7. Which of the twelve safeguards to moral purity (page 208) did you find particularly helpful or challenging? Why?

Tip 

If both men and women are present in your group, you may wish to divide them for the remaining discussion and prayer time.

8. Read 1 Thessalonians 4:1–10 aloud. Discuss some of the insights about moral purity found in this passage. Here are some questions to get you started:

When Paul says we should "abstain from sexual immorality," what do you think is included?

Why do you think God takes sexual immorality so seriously?

Seeking Him Together

Paul "urged" the Thessalonians to be morally pure and "solemnly warned" them about sexual immorality. What responsibility do we have toward other believers when it comes to this matter of moral purity?

How does sexual sin affect our relationship with others? with God?

As Christians, we are a family ("brothers"), we "know God," and He has given His Holy Spirit to us. How should those facts affect our sexual choices?

In what ways might God "avenge" moral impurity? How could the thought of future judgment motivate us to be morally pure?

Why do you think Paul follows this passage on sexual purity with an exhortation about *brotherly love* (vv. 9–10)? How is true love a protection against immorality?

Praying for Revival

Pair off in twos (men with men, women with women). Ask each other the following questions and respond as honestly as possible:

- Are you experiencing moral freedom and walking in sexual purity?
- Is there anything God has been speaking to you about in relation to your sexual purity? Are there any areas where you are struggling morally—thought life, relationships, behavior? What is your greatest battle morally?
- How did you respond to question 10 in Day 2 of this lesson (p. 197)?
- What can I do to encourage or help you in this area of your life?

Take time to pray for each other, asking God for His grace to be morally pure. If this is not something either of you struggles with, pray for your spouses and/or others in the group. Pray for any who may be battling temptation in this area. Ask God to guard each of your hearts and make and keep you pure for His glory.

Tip +

In sharing your heart with your prayer partner, be careful not to violate the confidence of any other person or to elaborate on shameful details.

Lesson 11

The Spirit-Filled Life:

God's Power in You

Whether you realize it or not, the Holy Spirit is actively involved in every dimension of your Christian life, from before the point of your conversion until you get to heaven. We were never intended to live our lives apart from Him. In fact we *cannot* live the Christian life apart from Him!

Christian maturity cannot be attained by trying harder or doing more. God has not dangled the prospect of an abundant life before us then set us loose in a maze to try to find our way through. The Holy Spirit acts as our guide and our companion—the One sent from heaven to lead us home. He enables us to obey God, empowers us to become like Jesus, and fills us with supernatural power for work and for witness. We should, therefore, learn how to listen to Him, how to follow Him, how to rely on His power, and how to walk in His fullness.

"Walk in the Spirit, and you shall not fulfill the lust of the flesh."
(Galatians 5:16 NKJV)

Psalm 139:7–12
John 14:15–17
1 Corinthians 2:10–13
2 Corinthians 5:1–5

Day 1: **Faith-Builder Story**

1 When did you first realize and understand that Christ died for your sin? How did that truth affect you? Write a brief account of your conversion experience.

Read the story about one woman's journey through the wilderness of depression and emotional instability into freedom and wholeness in Christ.

> Although my parents were professing Christians, the atmosphere in our home was characterized by strife, anger, and rebellion. As far back as I can remember, I experienced bouts with depression. During my early adult years my bitterness was fueled further by disappointments and failures in relationships.
>
> When I married and had children, I found that virtually every area of my life was negatively affected by bitterness and hurt. Peace, joy, and contentment always seemed to be beyond my grasp. I struggled to cope with life and its responsibilities, and came to a point where I was barely able to function. In the mornings it was all I could do to get my children up and dressed. Some days I couldn't get out of bed at all. However, because my husband held a prominent position in our church, I usually managed to make it on Sundays. I am amazed at how pride enabled me to do that in order to maintain the appearance of being okay.
>
> But inside the walls of our home, I was falling apart. My children and husband bore the brunt of my angry outbursts, periodic rage, and chronic depression. As a result of my emotional instability, our children began to grow up in a home much like the one in which I had been raised. I felt hopeless. I concluded that if this is all there was to life (and it seemed it was), then I wanted out. I just didn't see any purpose for going on.
>
> My husband, who seemed to be everything I was not (stable, consistent, "together"), tried very hard to meet my needs and help out. I began seeing a Christian psychiatrist, who prescribed a medication to deal

"I concluded that if this is all there was to life (and it seemed it was), then I wanted out."

with the depression. When that didn't seem to help, we tried another psychiatrist and a different medication. I received a great deal of sympathy and understanding. We went through various exercises designed to help me get over my hurt and painful memories. But nothing seemed to be able to help me change.

Several months and many dollars later, God brought a revival crusade team to our church. As the team ministered the simple truth of the Word of God, I began to see that I was not just a victim of the people and circumstances that had hurt me, but that I was personally responsible for the ways I had chosen to respond to those hurts.

For years I had blamed my family and others for my depression and my inability to cope with life. But God opened my eyes to see that many of those things I had called my "problems" were really sins against a holy God. I had willfully violated His Word through my bitterness, lack of forgiveness, and discontent, and through my refusal to "give thanks in everything."

God began to show me the revolting root of "self" in my life, with all of its many faces—self-pity, self-introspection, self-condemnation, self-centeredness, self-defense. On and on the list went. Self, self, self—that's what was at the root of my damaged mental and emotional condition. What a release it was to acknowledge that the circumstances of my past had not made me what I was; they had simply revealed the deep root of self that needed to be taken to the cross. Only then could I exchange my bitter, unforgiving self for the loving, sacrificial, forgiving life of Jesus.

"Self, self, self—that's what was at the root of my damaged mental and emotional condition."

Most of my life I had known I was supposed to walk in the Spirit, but I had never appropriated the power of the cross, which has freed me from the dominion of sin and self. I had appropriated the blood of Jesus to free me from the penalty of my sin, but I had never appropriated the fact that the cross frees me from the power of sin. I can now testify to the reality that walking in the Spirit means that by turning over the control of my life to Christ I can experience His freedom and power.[1]

2. What did this woman discover was at the root of her struggles with depression and emotional instability?

3. What helped this woman find freedom? What did not help?

4. Read John 7:37–39. How did Jesus describe what would take place as a result of the ministry of the Holy Spirit in our lives? If you have a desire or sense the need for a greater fullness of the Spirit in your life, express that to the Lord now in a simple written or verbal prayer.

Day 2: Truth Encounter

HELP FROM HEAVEN

The disciples were dejected. Jesus had just told them that He would be leaving them soon—departing not just to another place but to the other side of eternity. He had also told them that their lives would be extremely difficult. Because of their calling to be His disciples, many people would hate and reject them. They could not imagine the prospect of facing the future without their best Friend and spiritual leader. They needed comfort and reassurance. And that is exactly what Jesus gave them on their last evening together before He went to the cross, when He introduced them to the Holy Spirit.

> [6] *Because I have said these things to you, sorrow has filled your heart.*
> [7] *Nevertheless, I tell you the truth: it is to your advantage that I go away,*
> *for if I do not go away, the Helper will not come to you. But if I go, I will*
> *send him to you.* (John 16:6–7)

5 Knowing their deep sorrow, why could Jesus say to His disciples, "It is to your advantage that I go away"?

For more than thirty years, Christ had been the physical manifestation of God on earth. He was *Immanuel—God with us.* All along it had been the plan of God that after the Son gave His life sacrificially for our atonement and was raised from the dead, He would return to the Father's right hand. However, it was never in God's plan to leave His children alone. He always intended to be present with them.

That same evening, Jesus said to His disciples, "I will ask the Father, and he will give you another Helper, to be with you forever, even the Spirit of truth" (John 14:16). *I will never leave you nor forsake you* was not sentimentalism, it was God's promise—a promise He keeps to this day through the presence of the Holy Spirit, our constant Helper.

Key Point 

God is constantly with His children through the presence of the Holy Spirit.

Insight 

The Greek word for "Helper"is *parakletos,* describing one who is called to another's side to be an advocate, intercessor, and counselor. The same word is occasionally translated "comforter" in the New Testament.

Insight 

The Holy Spirit is not an "it." He is a divine person, a member of the Trinity. He is God, as Jesus is God, and is coequal with the Father and the Son (Matthew 28:19; Acts 5:3–4).

Day 2

6 What hope does the truth that God is with you and you are not alone give you today for your circumstances?

“Any emphasis upon the person and work of the Spirit that detracts from the person and work of Jesus Christ is not the Spirit's doing.”

—James Montgomery Boice

7 Which is more likely to happen: your problems will go away, or the Holy Spirit will comfort and strengthen you to pass through them? Explain your answer.

Not only did Jesus promise His disciples that God the Holy Spirit would be *with* them; He went on to say, “He dwells with you and will be *in you* (John 14:17; italics added).

8 God, in the form of the Holy Spirit, actually indwells every believer (see 1 Corinthians 3:16). What practical implications does that have for your life?

What does the Holy Spirit do in the life of a believer? Jesus made clear that the principal work of the Spirit would not be to glorify Himself but to put the spotlight on Christ and to make His truth known to us:

> 13 *When the Spirit of truth comes, he will guide you into all the truth, for he will not speak on his own authority, but whatever he hears he will speak, and he will declare to you the things that are to come.* 14 *He will glorify me, for he will take what is mine and declare it to you.* (John 16:13–14)

Day 2

9 The Holy Spirit came to make Christ more real to us—and more real to others through us. According to this passage, how does He do that?

10 From the time He convicts us of our need for Christ and draws us to faith in Christ, the Holy Spirit is actively involved in the life of every child of God. What do the following verses tell us about the ministry of the Spirit in our lives?

Ezekiel 36:27 _____
John 14:26; 16:13 _____
Acts 1:8 _____
Romans 5:5 _____
Romans 8:26–27 _____
Romans 15:13 _____
1 Corinthians 12:4–7, 11 _____
Galatians 5:22–23 _____

"Not a step can a believer advance without the Spirit. Not a victory can he achieve without the Spirit. Not a moment can he exist without the Spirit. As he needed Him at the first, so he needs Him all his journey through."

—Octavius Winslow

The indwelling Holy Spirit enables us to live a life of spiritual freedom, fullness, and fruitfulness. Select one of the items from this list and thank God for the way this particular work of the Holy Spirit affects your life today. Thank the Father for sending the Holy Spirit, and ask Him to glorify Christ—in you and through you.

Day 2

Day 3: Truth Encounter

GOD AT WORK IN ME

! Key Point

God's power is at work in us by the Holy Spirit.

Insight

Sanctification is the progressive work of God that frees us from sin's control and makes us more like Christ. Sanctification is initiated and sustained by the Holy Spirit within us and supported by the body of Christ — the church — around us.

Insight

In Scripture the word *flesh* describs the natural state of human beings apart from Christ. Even after a person receives Christ and is reborn by the Spirit of God, that person still dwells within the confines and influences of that flesh, and will until his earthly body is replaced with a heavenly one (1 Corinthians 15:50ff).

The Holy Spirit is actively involved in our salvation. Jesus said, "When he [the Holy Spirit] comes, he will convict the world concerning sin and righteousness and judgment" (John 16:8). It is the Holy Spirit who draws us to faith in Christ by first convicting us of our sinfulness.

After we are reborn, it is the Spirit who assures us of our standing with God: "The Spirit himself bears witness with our spirit that we are children of God" (Romans 8:16). That assurance is foundational to our victory in the battle against sin, our understanding of spiritual matters, and our pursuit of Christlikeness.

After becoming a child of God, we enter a process called *sanctification*—a process that continues until the day we arrive in heaven. This too is a work of the Holy Spirit:

> *And such were some of you. But you were washed, you were sanctified, you were justified in the name of the Lord Jesus Christ and by the Spirit of our God.* (1 Corinthians 6:11)

> *God from the beginning chose you for salvation through sanctification by the Spirit and belief in the truth.* (2 Thessalonians 2:13, NKJV)

11 Define *sanctification* in your own words.

Sanctification is a process whereby we are transformed into the likeness of Jesus. That process is not always easy. If you have been a Christian any length of time, you are aware that you are in a spiritual battle. Some of our enemies are external: Satan, God's eternal enemy, seeks to win our allegiance. The world system in which we live fights against everything that is godly. But we have a third and equally fierce enemy that is not external. If you are a child of God, there is a war going on *within* you—it is a battle between your natural flesh and the indwelling Spirit of God.

> *The desires of the flesh are against the Spirit, and the desires of the Spirit are against the flesh, for these are opposed to each other, to keep you from doing the things you want to do.* (Galatians 5:17)

Our natural flesh—with all its desires, thoughts, values, and behavior—is twisted, corrupt, and opposed to God. The Spirit of Christ living in us is in the process of transforming our desires into holy ones. But our flesh is powerful; it would rather thrive than die. So on the one hand, we feel the pull toward obedience and righteousness while also feeling the counterpull to appease our flesh with its cravings.

12 The following chart illustrates this battle by contrasting some of the heart attitudes that are characteristic of our flesh with the attitudes that are produced by the Spirit of God within us.
In each contrasting pair, place a check mark next to the one that most often characterizes your life.

Heart Attitudes of the Flesh	Heart Attitudes of the Spirit
❍ Gruff, abrasive, anxious	❍ Sweet-spirited, pleasant
❍ Stern, irritable, unmoved	❍ Tenderhearted
❍ Focused on self, impatient	❍ Kind
❍ Bitter, easily hurt, scornful	❍ Gentle
❍ Jealous, demanding	❍ Lowly in heart
❍ Proud, selfish	❍ Sacrificial
❍ Lazy, irresponsible, wants credit	❍ Servant's heart
❍ Enduring religion, critical	❍ Enjoying Christ
❍ Self-righteous	❍ Faith is a delight, not a duty
❍ Haughty, boastful, manipulative	❍ Poor in spirit
❍ Loose-tongued, judgmental	❍ Mourns with godly sorrow
❍ Unfriendly, wants own way	❍ Meek, yields rights
❍ Seeks own pleasure and comfort	❍ Hungers and thirsts for righteousness
❍ Unforgiving	❍ Merciful
❍ Loves self and worldly pleasure	❍ Pure in heart
❍ Gossip, stirs up strife	❍ Peacemaker
❍ Emotions controlled by circumstances	❍ Full of joy in the Lord

"Although there will always be some lingering influence of the flesh until we meet the Lord, we have no excuse for sin to continue to corrupt our lives....We have the resources of the Spirit of Christ within us to resist and put to death the deeds of the body, which result from living according to the flesh."

—John MacArthur

Ultimately, the battle between the flesh and the Spirit is a battle for control. Based on the exercise above, do you live your life more under the control of the flesh or the Spirit?

The Spirit places within every child of God a desire to be free from the control of the flesh. But is that really possible? Many Christians spend much of their lives *struggling* and *trying harder* to repress their fleshly tendencies. The problem is: *flesh can't reform flesh.* Our fleshly passions and desires need to be put to death. In Romans 8, Paul calls us to live according to the Spirit, who alone has the power to overcome our flesh:

> [5] *For those who live according to the flesh set their minds on the things of the flesh, but those who live according to the Spirit set their minds on the things of the Spirit.* [6] *To set the mind on the flesh is death, but to set the mind on the Spirit is life and peace....*
>
> [12] *So then, brothers, we are debtors, not to the flesh, to live according to the flesh.* [13] *For if you live according to the flesh you will die, but if by the Spirit you put to death the deeds of the body, you will live.* (Romans 8:5–6, 12–13)

13 According to these verses from Romans 8, what action is required on our part in the battle between the Spirit and the flesh (vv. 6, 13)?

14 In an average day, do you spend more time thinking about spiritual truth or about giving your flesh what it wants? What are some ways we can set our minds on the Spirit instead of on the flesh?

The pull of our flesh is strong. But the Spirit is even more powerful. We must exercise faith in the power of the indwelling Holy Spirit to grant us victory over the flesh.

15 Read Romans 8:11. How much power does the Holy Spirit have? What is the implication of that truth as you face the daily battle between your flesh and the Spirit?

"Although the Christian life is warfare, it is warfare in which victory is always possible."

—John MacArthur

Day 3

Day 4: Truth Encounter

WALKING BY THE SPIRIT

! Key Point

Every believer is to be filled with the Spirit—not occasionally but continually.

Paul urged the Christians in Ephesus to be *filled with* the Holy Spirit (Ephesians 5:18). Similarly, he exhorted the Galatians to walk by the Spirit:

> [16] *But I say, walk by the Spirit, and you will not gratify the desires of the flesh.... [25] If we live by the Spirit, let us also walk by the Spirit.* (Galatians 5:16, 25)

In both cases, Paul was challenging believers to yield to the control of the Holy Spirit, not just for a short time but every moment of their lives. Having faced some of life's harshest circumstances and the pull of his own sinful flesh, Paul knew that living under the Spirit's control was the only true way to live victoriously. And he wanted those whom he loved to experience the same.

"The Spirit-filled life is not a special, deluxe edition of Christianity. It is part and parcel of the total plan of God for His people."

—A. W. Tozer

16 Why do you think so many Christians are *not* consistently filled with (do not walk by) the Holy Spirit?

Due to the abuses and excesses we may have observed, we may be skeptical, even fearful, of where a discussion about the fullness of the Spirit will lead. Or we may prefer to maintain control of our life, not wanting to be filled with or led by anyone but ourselves. Sadly, many believers are simply unfamiliar with what the Scripture teaches about the fullness of the Spirit.

The Scripture uses the simile of drunkenness to help us understand that to be filled with the Holy Spirit is to be under His control.

> *And do not get drunk with wine, for that is debauchery, but be filled with the Spirit.* (Ephesians 5:18)

17 How does the word picture of being "drunk with wine" shed light on what it means to be "filled with the Spirit"?

18 After commanding us to be filled with the Spirit (Ephesians 5:18), Paul describes what that looks like in everyday life. Read the following verses and list some of the practical evidences of being filled with the Spirit.

In our public worship (Ephesians 5:19–20)

In our relationships with other believers (Ephesians 5:21)

In the marriage relationship (Ephesians 5:22–25)

In parent/child relationships (Ephesians 6:1–4)

In the workplace (Ephesians 6:5–9)

In our spiritual warfare (Ephesians 6:10–18)

Day 4

> "Blessed Spirit of the Lord, forgive us that we have done such despite to you, by our forgetfulness of you, by our proud self-sufficiency, by resisting your influences, and quenching your fire!"
>
> —C. H. Spurgeon

19 According to the Scriptures, the Holy Spirit can be grieved (Ephesians 4:30); He can be quenched (1 Thessalonians 5:19); and He can be resisted (Acts 7:51). What are some ways we might grieve or quench the Spirit—some things that could hinder the free flow of God's life, power, and joy in and through us? (Ephesians 4:30–32 names several.)

20 Is there anything in your life right now that is grieving or quenching the Spirit and preventing you from walking by the Spirit? Some unconfessed sin? An unresolved conflict with another believer? Some point of disobedience or resistance? Unbelief? Self-sufficiency?

Every time we say yes to our flesh and no to God, we grieve His Spirit and give greater control over to our flesh. Likewise, each act of obedience and surrender to God puts us more fully under the control of the Holy Spirit and releases His power in our lives. This simple truth is fundamental to walking in the Spirit—simply obeying Him each moment of the day. When we do sin, and we will, we should quickly confess our sin and surrender afresh to His control.

Day 4

Are you filled with the Holy Spirit right now? You can be. Being filled with the Spirit is not some sort of mystical experience reserved for certain Christians who are especially privileged or extraspiritual. It simply involves confessing any and all known sin, walking in moment-by-moment obedience to His leadership, and relying on Him to live His life through us (Galatians 2:20). As we are filled with the Spirit, His supernatural power will be released in and through our lives—granting victory over sin and our flesh, producing in us the heart and character of the Lord Jesus, and empowering us for effective witness and service.

Ask God to fill you with His Spirit. Trust Him to do it. Then thank Him for the incredible gift of the Spirit.

"The Spirit-filled life is a life of absolute, unconditional, unquestioning obedience to God."

—Del Fehsenfeld Jr.

Day 5: Making It Personal

When we are filled with the Spirit and living under His control, He will produce in us what the Scripture calls "the fruit of the Spirit":

> [22] *The fruit of the Spirit is love, joy, peace, patience, kindness, goodness, faithfulness,* [23] *gentleness, self-control; against such things there is no law.* (Galatians 5:22–23)

This fruit is really a description of the Lord Jesus Himself—the One the Spirit came to glorify! These graces or qualities will be evident in the life of a person who is living under the control of the Holy Spirit.

Take time to read and meditate on one or more of the Scriptures next to each quality below. Then prayerfully consider the questions that follow. As you do, ask the Spirit to reveal the true inclination of your heart; ask Him to produce His fruit in and through your life.

Love (1 Corinthians 13:4–8a; 1 John 4:7–12)

- Do people feel they have to gain my approval, or do they generally know that I love them and that I will help them in any way I can?
- Am I more driven to give love or to receive it?
- Do I genuinely love those people in my life who are unlovable or who do not love me in return?

Insight

Got joy? Five times in the New Testament—Acts 13:52; Romans 14:17; 15:13; Galatians 5:22; 1 Thessalonians 1:6—joy is attributed to the presence of the Holy Spirit.

Joy (Psalm 4:7; 16:11; 32:11; John 15:11; Philippians 4:4)

- Is my level of joy and happiness usually consistent, regardless of external circumstances or how others treat me?
- Do people see the joy of the Lord displayed in my life?
- Do I "serve the Lord with gladness"?

Peace (John 14:27; 16:33; Philippians 4:6–7; Colossians 3:15; 2 Thessalonians 3:16)

- When I am under pressure, is my spirit generally calm, rather than frantic or turbulent?
- Do I exhibit an inner tranquility of mind and a quiet confidence that God is in control, regardless of what is going on around me?

Patience (Colossians 1:11–12; James 1:2–4; 5:8)

- Am I long-suffering when I am mistreated by others?
- Am I willing to accept and endure irritating and adverse circumstances?
- Am I willing to wait for God to vindicate me or to reward my labors?

Kindness (Ephesians 4:32; 2 Timothy 2:24)

- Do I treat others as I wish to be treated by them and as God has treated me?
- Do I demonstrate genuine concern for others?
- Am I thoughtful, considerate, and alert to the needs of others?

Goodness (Luke 6:27b; Romans 12:21; Galatians 6:10)

- Do I manifest kindness by doing good works for fellow believers?
- Do I seek to overcome evil by actively doing good to those who wrong or hate me?

Faithfulness (Matthew 24:45–46; Luke 16:10–13; 1 Corinthians 4:2; 15:58)

- Am I committed to making choices that please God, even when I know others aren't watching me?
- Do I stick with a job or task until it is completed in the manner it should be?
- Am I dependable? Trustworthy? Loyal?

Gentleness (Meekness) (Matthew 5:5; 11:29; Ephesians 4:1–2; Titus 3:2; James 3:17; 1 Peter 3:4)

- Am I easy to approach, even about difficult matters, or do others have legitimate reason to dread conversations with me?
- Do I endure misunderstanding and injustice without retaliating or being defensive?
- Do I have a yielded, teachable spirit?

Self-control (1 Corinthians 9:24–27; Titus 2:1–10)

- Am I temperate and disciplined in matters of food and drink? In the use of my tongue? In my use of time? In my reactions and responses to people and circumstances?
- Are my natural passions and appetites under the control of the Holy Spirit?

After working through an exercise like this one (or others in this study), you may feel concerned, even overwhelmed, by the spiritual progress you need to make. Remember that these are not *natural* qualities we can manufacture...they are the *supernatural* "fruit" that will be produced in our lives as we are filled with the Spirit of Christ. These are the qualities of His life flowing through us as we abide in Him and surrender to His control. God has not left you to do this on your own. By the Spirit He has taken up residence in you and is constantly at work sanctifying you.

---

[1] The Faith-Builder story in Lesson 11 is adapted from "Free Through Christ," *Spirit of Revival*, vol. 22, no. 1, March 1992, pp. 7–10, published by Life Action Ministries.

Day 5

Seeking Him Together

Opening It Up

1. What insight about the person and work of the Holy Spirit did you find particularly helpful or encouraging in this lesson?

> "We must have the Holy Spirit's power and presence, otherwise our religion will become a mockery before God, and a misery to ourselves."
>
> —C. H. Spurgeon

2. Tell the group about a specific way that the Holy Spirit has helped you or is helping you to grow in your faith in Christ.

Talking It Over

3. The Faith-Builder story was about a woman who struggled with depression and anger. How do you think the act of seeking forgiveness from God, her husband, and others for the way her sin had affected them contributed to this woman's healing?

Seeking Him Together

"The Spirit in every believer is a deep and living well of all spiritual blessings."
—Octavius Winslow

4. Even if we are hurt deeply by the way others treat us, why is it essential to accept responsibility for our responses rather than embracing a "victim mentality"?

5. List some of the things the Holy Spirit does in the life of a Christian.

6. What does *sanctification* mean? What is God's role and what is our responsibility in the process of sanctification?

"The Spirit-filled life is the Christ-directed life by which Christ lives His life in and through us in the power of the Holy Spirit."
—Bill Bright

7. How does the Holy Spirit help us overcome our flesh?

8. What does it mean to be filled with the Holy Spirit? Describe a person who is walking in, or filled with, the Holy Spirit.

9. Discuss the impact of believers *not* being filled with the Spirit—in their homes? In our churches? In our society?

10. What do you think might be the impact if all believers began to be filled with and walk in the Spirit—in their homes? In our churches? In our society?

Praying for Revival

Pray together as a group or with one or two others. Ask God to help each of you to come under and remain under the control of the Holy Spirit. Ask Him for a fresh filling of His Spirit in your life. Cry out to Him for a revival of Spirit-filled living in your home, your church, and your community.

The Personal Devotional Life: "Seeking Him" Daily

What if someone told you that one year from now you could look back over twelve months of consistent spiritual growth? You could be walking more closely with God than ever before. You could be enjoying a deeper awareness of His love for you and your love for Him. You could be walking in greater freedom over sin. Your life could be bearing the fruit of the Spirit and God would be using you as an instrument of His grace in others' lives.

Would you want that? These are not pipe dreams; they are the fruit we bear as we grow in intimacy with God. In this final lesson, we want to consider one of the most important keys to ongoing personal revival. That key is what is known as *a personal devotional life—the practice of spending time alone each day with God, in His Word and in prayer.*

The Christian's devotional life is foundational to his or her spiritual maturity and capacity to know God and to make Him known to others. A personal devotional life involves more than just "having devotions." It is a call to *devotion*—an opportunity to cultivate an intimate love relationship with God. It is vital to a lifetime of "seeking Him" and experiencing the joy of personal revival.

MEMORY VERSE

"One thing have I asked of the Lord, that will I seek after: that I may dwell in the house of the Lord all the days of my life, to gaze upon the beauty of the Lord and to inquire in his temple." (Psalm 27:4)

Psalm 63:1–8; 119:33–40
Matthew 6:5–15
2 Timothy 3:14–4:5

Day 1: Faith-Builder Story

1 How would you define or describe what it means to have a "personal devotional life"?

This week's Faith-Builder story is an account that Tim Grissom wrote about his wife, Janiece, shortly before she was diagnosed with Lou Gehrig's Disease in 1999 (the disease took her life eleven months later).

> One of my friends teases me by saying that I married "way over my head." He's right. I often wonder why God has blessed me with such a wonderful soul mate. My wife is kind, fun loving, hospitable, and generous. She doesn't grumble about what we don't have, and she expresses genuine appreciation for what we do have.
>
> There is one quality, however, that stands head and shoulders above all her other precious qualities—she walks intimately with God. I'm not referring to a kind of heavenly, holier-than-thou swagger; I mean that she simply obeys God. She listens to what He says and then does it. That's not to say that she doesn't have spiritual struggles, but when she does, she doesn't blame her circumstances or become moody. She asks God to search her heart, and she waits for His answer.
>
> I, on the other hand, have often resisted God. I'm well acquainted with stubbornness and pride, and I'm not fully out of their grip yet. But my life began to change a few years ago. Much of my turning back to God came as the result of my wife's consistent example of godliness.
>
> There are reasons my wife is who she is. Years ago she attended a church youth camp, where she was challenged to read her Bible every day for one year. When my wife makes a promise, she is bound by her word to keep it. So when she made that commitment before God, she meant business. My wife was in junior high school then. In the two decades that we have been married, I have never known her to miss a single day of having her "quiet time" with God. Not one.
>
> I don't say these things to put my wife on a pedestal. She's not perfect, of course. My point is that faithfully taking a few minutes each day to meet with God in His Word and prayer has formed her into a godly

woman. And her life "won" me over. If she had nagged or manipulated or ridiculed me about my spiritual growth, she would have only succeeded in driving me away from wanting to grow in Christ. Instead, she lived a very real life of simple faith and devotion to Christ. And it made me thirsty for what she had.

"In the two decades that we have been married, I have never known her to miss a single day of having her 'quiet time' with God."

I know that many people have gripping stories and dramatic events surrounding their experience of personal revival. It wasn't like that for me. God got my attention over a period of time, and it has been just as real and life-changing. Along with my wife, God has brought other people across my path who have challenged and helped me grow spiritually. The key element, however, has been the regular intake of His Word, especially in my personal devotional time.

"God's Word has become…a thing we simply cannot do without."

God's Word has been like a medicine to reduce my anger, worry, and impatience. It has acted as a map in helping our family make decisions or reroute our ill-advised plans. It has provided light to reveal snares that were sometimes hiding in the shadows. God's Word has become for us a thing we simply cannot do without.

I thank God for a youth speaker who encouraged a group of junior high campers to read their Bibles. I thank God for a young lady who made that commitment and kept it. I thank God for His Word and how He has used our daily appointments to draw me nearer to Him.[1]

2 What qualities did this wife develop—as a result of her faithfulness to read God's Word—that caused her husband to want to grow in Christ?

Day 1

Psalm 42 is the prayer of a man who is desperate for God:

> [1] *As a deer pants for flowing streams,*
> *so pants my soul for you, O God.*
> [2] *My soul thirsts for God, for the living God.*
> *When shall I come and appear before God?. . . .*
> [8] *By day the Lord commands his steadfast love,*
> *and at night his song is with me,*
> *a prayer to the God of my life.* (vv. 1–2, 8)

3 How thirsty are you for God? What keeps you from "coming before Him" more often than you do?

Day 1

Day 2: Truth Encounter

FIRST THINGS FIRST

In spite of all our time-saving devices and modern technology, many people today struggle with feeling perpetually hurried, frazzled, stressed-out, over-busy, over-committed, and overwhelmed.

This week's memory verse (Psalm 27:4) is the testimony of a man (King David) whose life was anchored in a steadfast determination: "If I don't get anything else accomplished in my day, the *one thing* I will pursue above all else is to know God and develop a relationship with Him."

In a familiar passage in Luke's gospel, we encounter two sisters, one of whom understood (and the other needed to learn) the importance of keeping "first things first." Read the passage below and then meditate on it by answering the questions that follow:

> 38 *Now it happened as they went that He entered a certain village; and*
> *a certain woman named Martha welcomed Him into her house.* 39 *And*
> *she had a sister called Mary, who also sat at Jesus' feet and heard His word.*
>
> 40 *But Martha was distracted with much serving, and she approached Him and said, "Lord, do You not care that my sister has left me to serve alone? Therefore tell her to help me."*
>
> 41 *And Jesus answered and said to her, "Martha, Martha, you are wor-*
> *ried and troubled about* ***many things.*** 42 *But* ***one thing*** *is needed, and*
> *Mary has chosen that good part, which will not be taken away from her."* (Luke 10:38–42, NKJV, emphasis added)

Key Point !

Cultivating an intimate relationship with God should be the number one priority for every believer and requires taking time to "sit at Jesus' feet" and "listen to His Word."

4 How were Martha's priorities different from Mary's priorities?

"My spirit has become dry because it forgets to feed on You."

—John of the Cross

5 How did Martha's priorities and choices affect her response to pressure, to her family, and to Jesus?

Day 2

> "This perpetual hurry of business and company ruins me in soul if not in body. More solitude and earlier hours! . . . Surely the experience of all good men confirms the proposition that without a due measure of private devotions, the soul will grow lean."
>
> —William Wilberforce

6 What is the "one thing" Mary chose that, according to Jesus, is the only absolutely necessary priority?

7 What are some of the symptoms that we may have been neglecting our personal relationship with Jesus? What can we do about it?

8 Martha was distracted, "pulled apart," by all her meal preparations. What are some of the things that distract you and keep you from "sitting at the feet of Jesus and listening to Him"?

9 Check the following words/phrases that best describe your personal devotional life *prior* to starting this study.

- ❍ Nonexistent or sporadic
- ❍ A chore
- ❍ An obligation
- ❍ Going through the motions
- ❍ A duty
- ❍ Dry
- ❍ Routine
- ❍ Consistent
- ❍ A joy
- ❍ A privilege
- ❍ Spiritual lifeline
- ❍ A delight
- ❍ Spiritually nourishing
- ❍ Intimate fellowship with God

Day 2

10 If you checked any boxes on the left side, identify some of the obstacles that have kept you from developing a meaningful devotional life.

- Too busy
- Difficulty concentrating
- Too many distractions
- No real desire
- Don't know how
- Didn't realize the need
- I get my spiritual nourishment from church, attending a Bible study, or the media (Christian radio, TV, or the Internet)
- Other: ____________________

11 What changes do you need to make in your schedule, your lifestyle, or your priorities to allow you to spend adequate time "sitting at the feet of Jesus, listening to Him speak"?

Getting Started in a Personal Devotional Life

The whole idea of spending time alone with God each day may be new to you. Or it may be something you have done in the past. Here are some suggestions to help you develop (or restart) a daily devotional time with God.

> **Set the priority.** Don't try to squeeze your personal devotional time into an already overcrowded schedule; instead, start planning your day around your time with the Lord.

Make the commitment. If we don't do it today, we probably won't do it tomorrow…or next week…or next month. Soon another year will have passed, and we will have missed all those opportunities for spending time alone with God and developing an intimate relationship with Him. As you begin taking steps to develop a consistent devotional life, find someone you trust and ask him or her to hold you accountable to your commitment. Share what God is teaching you and how you are growing through your time with Him.

A 30-Day Challenge

If you have made it this far in *Seeking Him,* you have already been enjoying some of the benefits of consistent time in God's presence. Continuing your personal devotional time is crucial to sustaining the work God has been doing in your heart through the course of this study and to enjoying an even deeper level of intimacy with Him in the days ahead.

Whether you already have an established devotional habit or are just getting started, consider making the following commitment:

> *By God's grace, out of a desire to know Him more intimately, I purpose to spend some time alone with the Lord in His Word and in prayer, every day for the next thirty days.*
>
> Signed ______________________________
>
> Date ______________________________

"A man can no more take in a supply of grace for the future than he can eat enough for the next six months, or take sufficient air into his lungs at one time to sustain life for a week. We must draw upon God's boundless store of grace from day to day as we need it."

—D. L. Moody

Be consistent. Many people have discovered that it is ideal (though not necessarily easy!) to start the day in the Word and prayer, before their minds are drawn into other activities and responsibilities. There is ample precedent in Scripture for a "morning quiet time." However, the time of day is not as important as consistency. Select a time and setting where you can meet God regularly and won't be easily interrupted or distracted.

Choose a plan. Many helpful books and devotional guides are available at your local Christian bookstore or even at the public library. One of these tools or some type of Bible reading plan may help you get started. Your pastor or a respected Christian friend may offer suggestions. Find a plan, method, or tool that works best for you based on your makeup, season of life, and spiritual maturity. (You'll find some simple suggestions in the Day 4: "Making It Personal" section.)

Integrate other activities. Your devotional life should consistently include time in the Word, prayer, and worship. However, at times, you may want to incorporate other activities, such as:

- keeping a journal
- praying about and making important decisions
- writing notes of thanks and encouragement
- arranging or rearranging your schedule (praying about what to do and when)
- singing hymns and praise choruses
- giving to others (determining what, how much, to whom, and so forth)
- memorizing Scripture

Day 3: **Truth Encounter**

THE WORD OF GOD

Those who love and follow God's Word will be blessed—that is the theme of Psalm 119.

> *1 Blessed are those whose way is blameless,*
> *who walk in the law of the Lord!*
> *2 Blessed are those who keep his testimonies,*
> *who seek him with their whole heart,*

Insight

The longest chapter in the Bible, Psalm 119 is a warm tribute to the Word of God. Each stanza has eight lines, each of which starts with the same letter of the Hebrew alphabet. The twenty-two stanzas form an acrostic, using the twenty-two letters of the Hebrew alphabet consecutively.

12 Circle the words in the verses above that describe the response we should have to God and to His Word.

13 What do each of the following verses from Psalm 119 tell us about the benefits or blessings we can derive from God's Word?

Psalm 119	Blessings Found through God's Word
11 I have stored up your word in my heart, *that I might not sin against you.*	
24 Your testimonies are my . . . counselors.	
28 My soul melts away for sorrow; *strengthen me according to your word!*	
47 I find my delight in your commandments, *which I love.*	
98 Your commandment makes me wiser *than my enemies,* *for it is ever with me.*	
103 How sweet are your words to my taste, *sweeter than honey to my mouth!*	
104 Through your precepts I get understanding; *therefore I hate every false way.*	

In Ezra, we find a biblical example of a man who was intentional about getting to know God through His Word. According to Ezra 7:10, this was not something he took lightly:

> *Ezra had set his heart to **study** the Law of the Lord, and to do it and to **teach** his statutes and rules in Israel* (emphasis added).

14 What three things did Ezra set his heart to do in relation to the Word of God?

Ezra was a godly man who led a group of Jews from their exile in Persia back to their homeland in Jerusalem (ca. 458 B.C.). Trained as a scribe of the law, he called God's people back to the Word of God. The revival that resulted is recorded in Nehemiah 8–10.

Ezra did not have a casual attitude toward God's Word. He was serious about studying and meditating on it, obeying it, and reproducing it in the lives of others.

15 How does Ezra's heart for God's Word compare with your attitude toward the Word? Is your heart set toward the Word of God? Which of these three things above do you need to set your heart to do more consistently?

Key Point !

Consistent intake of Scripture into our minds, hearts, and lives is essential to sustain spiritual life.

A consistent intake of Scripture (reading, memorizing, meditating, studying, etc.) can have both a corrective and a preventive result. God's Word can instruct us, confront wrong thinking or behavior, correct and redirect us when we're wayward, and equip us for service in His kingdom (2 Timothy 3:16–17). The whole of humankind's accumulated knowledge cannot compare to the pure and plain wisdom of God's holy Word.

Above all, it is through the written Word, illuminated by the Spirit of God, that we come to know Christ, the Living Word, in a deep and personal way. Your relationship with Christ will never be any greater

> "Nothing can be more healthful to the soul of the believer than feeding upon the Word, and digesting it by frequent meditation."
>
> —C. H. Spurgeon

than your relationship with His Word! What a loss it is to deprive ourselves of the abundant riches that are readily available in His Word.

Reading God's Word is the starting place for developing a growing relationship with Him. But Ezra's life illustrates that we need to do more than just *read* the Word.

16 According to the following verses, what else is needed in order for the Word to have the maximum impact and effect in our lives?

Joshua 1:8; Psalm 1:2 ______

Psalm 119:56; Ezekiel 33:31–32; James 1:22 ______

Hebrews 4:2 ______

17 Write a brief prayer thanking God for His Word and expressing your heart's desire to be filled with His Word and to enjoy rich fellowship with Him through His Word.

Day 4: **Making It Personal**

Take time today to do what Mary did in Luke 10—to sit at Jesus' feet and listen to His Word. You may already have a method or plan selected to guide you in your personal devotions. If not, the following suggestions can help you get started. Of course, don't feel obligated to follow this outline. There is no "right way" to have your devotional time—remember, the goal is to cultivate a relationship with God, not to check your devotions off your "to do" list! [2]

> "There is greater rest and solace to be found in the presence of God for one hour, than in an eternity of the presence of man."
>
> —Robert Murray M'Cheyne

A. Prepare Your Heart

- "Enter his gates with thanksgiving, and his courts with praise!" (Psalm 100:4). Worship Him; praise Him for who He is; express thanksgiving for what He has done.
- Ask God to show you anything that could hinder your fellowship and communion with Him. Confess any sin He brings to mind.
- Ask God to quiet your heart, to open your ears, and to speak to you through His Word. Ask His Holy Spirit to be your Teacher. Commit yourself to obey whatever He shows you. You may want to pray these prayers from Scripture:

Open my eyes that I may see
Wonderful things in your law.
Give me understanding,
And I will keep your law
And obey it with all my heart. (Psalm 119:18, 34 NIV)

Show me your ways, O Lord,
Teach me your paths;
Guide me in your truth and teach me,
For you are God my Savior,
And my hope is in you all day long. (Psalm 25:4–5 NIV)

That which I see not teach thou me:
If I have done iniquity,
I will do no more. (Job 34:32 KJV)

Day 4

"The first three years after conversion, I neglected the Word of God. Since I began to search it diligently, the blessing has been wonderful. I have read the Bible through one hundred times and always with increasing delight!"

—George Mueller

"Remember that it is not hasty reading, but serious meditation on holy and heavenly truths, that makes them prove sweet and proftable to the soul."

—Thomas Brooks

B. Listen to God

Select a chapter or a passage of Scripture. (Ideally, make a practice of reading consecutively through entire books or sections of the Bible in your devotional time.) Read through the passages thoughtfully and prayerfully. Underline or highlight key words, phrases, or verses that stand out to you.

There are many different approaches to reading and meditating on Scripture. Here's a simple method that many people have found useful. (Even children can do this, some as young as nine or ten.) All you need is your Bible, a pen, and a blank notebook or journal (or you may prefer to use your computer).

The "S-A" (Summary-Application) Method: Write your own brief "commentary" on the Scripture. As you read each chapter, record the following:

- *Summary:* One or two sentences summarizing the chapter ("What does this passage say?")
- *Application:* One or two sentences of personal application, expressing how something in that chapter can be applied to your life; how it spoke to you personally. ("What does this passage mean for me? What should I do?") The application should be personal and might include promises to claim, warnings to heed, truths to obey, attitudes or behavior to adjust, and so on.

C. Respond to God

A meaningful devotional life is a dialogue; we allow God to "speak" through His Word and the promptings of His Holy Spirit. Then we respond to Him with love, gratitude, faith, surrender, and obedience. Prayer allows us to commune with God through praise, thanksgiving, confession of sin, petition for our needs, and intercession for the needs of others. Our devotional life can become the time and place where our most important decisions are made. What better place than in the quiet, holy, secure, and intimate presence of our heavenly Father?

Day 4

During and/or following your time in the Word, respond to God in prayer and praise:

1. Agree with Him about what He has revealed to you in His Word. Surrender your will to obey His commands and to follow through with any steps He is leading you to take; confess any sin He has shown you; claim any promises He has made through His Word.

2. Praise and worship Him for what He has revealed about His heart, character, and ways.

3. Bring your needs before Him. Ask God to show you how to pray for those needs in accordance with His will, as it is revealed in His Word.

4. Bring the needs of others before Him. As He prompts, pray for your family, church, community, nation, and the advancement of His kingdom throughout the world.

Close your time today by personalizing this week's memory verse and praying it back to the Lord:

> *One thing have I asked of the Lord, that will I seek after: that I may dwell in the house of the Lord all the days of my life, to gaze upon the beauty of the Lord and to inquire in his temple.* (Psalm 27:4)

Day 5: Where To from Here?

SEEKING HIM FOR CONTINUOUS REVIVAL

"You who seek God, let your hearts revive" (Psalm 69:32b). Have you been "seeking Him" through the course of this study? If so, God has promised to revive your heart! You may already be experiencing many of the blessings and joys of personal revival.

How has God revived your heart through this study? Take time to consider and record your response to that question. (If you are going through this study with a group, you will have an opportunity to share your answer when you meet together.)

Where were you spiritually when you started *Seeking Him*? How has God changed you? Is there a particular truth (e.g., humility, honesty, clear conscience, forgiveness, sexual purity) that has especially affected your life? Explain.

At this point you may be wondering, *Where do I go from here? I don't want to lose the revival God has begun in my heart over the past twelve weeks.*

! Key Point

Whatever it takes to *get* revival is what it takes to *keep* it.

Remember this: Whatever it takes to get revival is what it takes to keep it. The basic truths that God has been using to set you free during these past weeks—humility, repentance, honesty, holiness, obedience, clear conscience, forgiveness, walking in the Spirit—are the same truths that will enable you to experience continuous revival.

That's why it's important for you to keep going back to these same foundational principles—again and again and again—and to engraft them into your mind, heart, and life. Periodically review the key points in each lesson; go through the "Making It Personal" exercises from time to time, to make sure you are still walking in the truth that sets us free.

A list of recommended "Revival Resources" has been provided at the end of this book to help you grow in your understanding of personal and corporate revival, as well as related themes.

As you continue to walk with God, ask Him how you can be used as an instrument of revival. Find one or two like-hearted believers and begin to pray together for revival in your homes, your churches, your community, and in our world. Share with others what God is doing in your heart and life. Consider going through this study again with one or more people you know who have a desire to seek the Lord and to experience the joy of personal revival.

"We cannot organize revival, but we can set our sails to catch the wind from Heaven when God chooses to blow upon His people once again."

—G. Campbell Morgan

A Benediction

> [20] *Now to him who is able to do far more abundantly than all that we ask or think, according to the power at work within us,* [21] *to him be glory in the church and in Christ Jesus throughout all generations, forever and ever. Amen.* (Ephesians 3:20–21)

How does this benediction encourage you regarding the ongoing process of revival in your life?

How does it give you hope as you pray and believe God for an outpouring of His Spirit in revival in our world?

---

[1] The Faith-Builder story in Lesson 12 is adapted from *A Place of Quiet Rest* by Nancy Leigh DeMoss (Chicago, Moody, 2002), pp. 259–60.

[2] For further practical assistance in developing a meaningful daily devotional life, see *A Place of Quiet Rest: Cultivating Intimacy with God Through a Daily Devotional Life* (© 2002, published by Moody), and *A 30-Day Walk with God in the Psalms* (© 2002, published by Moody), both by Nancy Leigh DeMoss.

Seeking Him **Together**

> "We Christians must simplify our lives or lose untold treasures on earth and in eternity. Modern civilization is so complex as to make the devotional life all but impossible. The need for solitude and quietness was never greater than it is today."
>
> —A. W. Tozer

Opening It Up

1. Do you generally identify more with Martha or Mary in the passage we considered in Luke 10? In what way(s)?

Talking It Over

2. Review the Faith-Builder story. What factors motivated Tim to make time with God and His Word a priority?

3. Can you think of someone whose example has been a challenge and motivation to you in this matter of a personal devotional life?

4. Based on what you have studied in this lesson, what are some of the positive benefits and blessings of having a consistent devotional life? Why does this need to be a priority for every believer?

5. What hurdles or obstacles have you experienced in relation to your personal devotional life? Share any practical insights that have been helpful to you in overcoming those obstacles and developing a meaningful devotional life.

6. Why is a personal devotional life so vital to experiencing ongoing personal revival?

"He who lives with little prayer—he who seldom looks up to heaven for a fresh influence from on high—he will be the man whose heart will become cold and barren."

—C. H. Spurgeon

7. Pair off with another person briefly (ideally someone you have prayed with earlier in this study), and share with each other any commitments you made while doing this lesson. Agree on how you can help hold each other accountable over the next thirty days for whatever God has put on your heart in relation to your personal devotional life.

8. Reconvene as a group for a time of rejoicing in God's goodness. How has God revived your heart and changed your life through this study? Is there a particular truth—humility, honesty, clear conscience, forgiveness, sexual purity, or other—that has especially impacted your life? Explain.

Seeking Him Together

Leader Tip

Save some time for this part so you won't be hurried in this closing time of sharing and prayer. Take advantage of this opportunity to rejoice in what God has been doing in your group and to open your hearts to each other and the Lord.

Praying for Revival

Spend some extended time in prayer—either as a whole group or in smaller groups of two to four people. Allow the Spirit to direct your prayer time. Pray brief prayers so all those who wish can pray aloud as many times as they are led.

- **PRAISE** God for what He has taught you about His heart and ways, and for what He has done in your hearts and lives over these weeks.
- **PRAY** for each other. Pray regarding any struggles you may be aware of that others are experiencing in their walk with God (use discretion). Pray that in the days ahead each person in your group will continue to seek the Lord and to experience the joy and freedom of personal revival.
- **PRAY** for a great moving of God's Spirit in genuine revival—in your homes, your church(s), in our nation, and throughout the world.

Suggestions for Group Leaders

If the discussion is going to flow smoothly and time is going to be well spent, each group needs a leader. That could be you. But don't worry! The leader for this kind of study is really more of a facilitator than a teacher. As a facilitator, you will provide suggestions and guidance to keep the group on track during the meeting. You will also raise questions to spark discussion.

If you've been designated the leader, consider enlisting an assistant or coleader to help you. This person can help with contacting members, give valuable feedback, and substitute for you if you must be absent. Or your group may decide to rotate leadership. This approach has some advantages if each leader is willing to put in the necessary time for preparation and prayer before the meeting.

For maximum effectiveness, group size should be limited to about ten or twelve members. With a small group like this, all members will have a chance to participate actively. If you have more than a dozen participants, consider dividing into two or more groups with a leader for each group. Groups may choose to meet in a church, a home, or some other setting. They may be made up of men only, of women only, or both together. If possible, allow ninety minutes (or more) for your discussion, sharing, and prayer time. If your situation does not allow the group to meet for that long, sessions can be shortened by the leader's selecting specific discussion questions from those provided.

Here are some suggestions to make your group time as effective and meaningful as possible:

1. **Be a group member as well as a leader.** Work through the material of each unit just as you expect every other member of your group to do. Allow God to work in your heart. Your greatest task in preparation is to be in a right relationship with God so you can know and follow the Holy Spirit's leadership.
2. **Try to make the total experience a warm and open one.** See that the meeting place is quiet, comfortable, and adequately lighted. Sit in a circle or around a table so that everyone can have eye contact. If time permits, provide refreshments and opportunity for people to interact more informally. Thoughtful touches like this can create a deeper intimacy among participants and make them look forward to coming back.
3. **Some of your group members may be unfamiliar with each other.** Keep this in mind, especially in the first few meetings, and try to get members to open up with one another and reach out in a friendly way. As the participants become more comfortable with each other, the discussion will go to a deeper level.
4. **Be sensitive.** Many of the topics covered in this book deal with deep, personal feelings and experiences as God works in people's hearts. These things are not always easy to share with others in a group setting, especially if members do not know each other well. Provide a warm, gracious atmosphere in which people can feel free to share or not share. Listen intently to what others say. Model openness and vulnerability balanced by tactfulness. Members should be assured of confidentiality in the group.
5. **Be prepared, but be flexible.** You should be equipped to lead the group through each segment and transition of the meeting, but allow the Holy Spirit to guide the session. You may come to a certain point during the discussion when it is obvious that God is working in an unusual way. Don't be in a hurry to move on. Allow God time and freedom to work.
6. **Feel free to adapt the material** to the particular situation of your group (including your available time frame). You may want to skip or revise some questions to better meet the needs of your group. Feel free to add specific examples or stories of your own that illustrate the truths emphasized in that week's lesson.

7. **Don't worry about silence after you ask a question.** Give members time to think about or formulate their responses. If the silence has gone on long enough or if the response is minimal, rephrase the question or ask a follow-up question.
8. After the first or second session, **ask for feedback from group members** whose wisdom you particularly value. Ask what you're doing well and where you could improve in your approach to leading the sessions. Then prayerfully plan to implement changes based on this constructive criticism.
9. **Pray for each session and each group member.** Trust God for revival and thank Him for it when it comes!

Revival **Resources**

This is by no means an exhaustive list of valuable resources on revival-related topics. Further, the inclusion of a resource on this list does not necessarily imply complete agreement with every point or an unqualified endorsement of the author, the resource, or the organization. Every believer should scrutinize all input (including this book) in the light of God's Word.

Books

Blackaby, Henry, and Claude V. King. *Experiencing God.* Nashville: Lifeway Christian Resources, 1993.

——. *Fresh Encounter.* Nashville: Broadman & Holman, 1997.

DeMoss, Nancy Leigh. Revive Our Hearts Series:

Brokenness: The Heart God Revives. Chicago: Moody, 2002.

Surrender: The Heart God Controls. Chicago: Moody, 2003.

Holiness: The Heart God Purifies. Chicago: Moody, 2004.

Duewel, Wesley L. *Ablaze for God.* Grand Rapids: Zondervan, 1989.

——. *Revival Fire.* Grand Rapids: Zondervan, 1995.

Edwards, Brian H. *Can We Pray for Revival?* Darlington, UK: Evangelical Press, 2001.

——. *Revival: A People Saturated with God.* Phillipsburg, NJ: P&R Press, 2004.

Edwards, Jonathan. *A Call to United, Extraordinary Prayer.* Great Britain, UK: Christian Focus Publications, 2003. (Christian Focus Publications are available in the US from STL-distributions.com; 1-800-289-2772.)

Fehsenfeld, Del, Jr. *Ablaze with His Glory.* Nashville: Thomas Nelson, 1993. (Available through Life Action Ministries.)

Hayden, Eric. *Praying for Revival: A Devotional on Model Prayers in the Bible.* Great Britain, UK: Christian Focus Publications, 2001.

Hession, Roy. *My Calvary Road.* Great Britain, UK: Christian Focus Publications, 1996.

———. *The Calvary Road.* Fort Washington, PA: Christian Literature Crusade, 1980.

———. *When I Saw Him . . . Where Revival Begins.* Fort Washington, PA: Christian Literature Crusade, 1982.

Hession, Roy, and Revel Hession. *We Would See Jesus.* Fort Washington, PA: Christian Literature Crusade, 1997 (revised edition).

Kaiser, Walter C., Jr. *Revive Us Again: Biblical Insights for Encouraging Spiritual Renewal.* Great Britain, UK: Christian Focus Publications, 2001.

Lewis, H. Elvet, G. Campbell Morgan, and I. V. Neprah. Richard Owen Roberts, ed. *Glory Filled the Land: A Trilogy on the Welsh Revival, 1904–1905.* Wheaton, IL: International Awakening, 1989.

Life Action Ministries. *Search My Heart.* Buchanan, MI: Life Action Ministries. (A loose-leaf collection of nearly forty "Making It Personal" worksheets reprinted from *Spirit of Revival* magazine. Designed to help you take personal inventory of your walk with God. May be reproduced for use by local churches, small groups, and individuals.)

Lloyd-Jones, D. Martyn. *Revival.* Wheaton, IL: Good News Publishers, 1987.

Moore, T. M. *Preparing Your Church for Revival.* Great Britain, UK: Christian Focus Publications, 2001.

Murray, Iain H. *Pentecost—Today? The Biblical Basis for Understanding Revival.* Edinburgh, UK: Banner of Truth Trust, 1998.

———. *Revival and Revivalism: The Making and Marring of American Evangelicalism 1750–1858.* Edinburgh, UK: Banner of Truth, 1994.

Orr, J. Edwin. *Campus Aflame: A History of Evangelical Awakenings in Collegiate Communities.* Wheaton, IL: International Awakening, 1994.

———. *The Event of the Century: The 1857–1858 Awakening.* Wheaton, IL: International Awakening, 1989.

———. *My All, His All.* Wheaton, IL: International Awakening, 1989.

Ortlund, Raymond. *When God Comes to Church: A Biblical Model for Revival Today.* Grand Rapids, MI: Baker Book House, 2000.

Phillips, Richard D. *Turning Back the Darkness: The Biblical Pattern of Reformation.* Wheaton, IL: Crossway Books, 2002.

Pratney, Winkie, ed. *Revival: Principles to Change the World.* Christian Life Books, 2002.

Ravenhill, Leonard. *Revival God's Way.* Minneapolis: Bethany, 1983.

———. *Why Revival Tarries.* Minneapolis: Bethany, 2004.

Roberts, Richard Owen. *Revival.* Wheaton, IL: Richard Owen Roberts Publishers, 1997.

———. *Sanctify the Congregation: A Call to the Solemn Assembly and to Corporate Repentance.* Wheaton, IL: International Awakening, 1994.

Tracy, Joseph. *The Great Awakening: A History of the Revival of Religion in the Time of Edwards and Whitefield.* Edinburgh, UK: Banner of Truth, 1989.

Booklets

Campbell, Duncan. *The Price and Power of Revival: Lessons from the Hebrides Awakening.* Vinton, VA: Christ Life Publications Classic Reprints. (www.christlifemin.org)

DeMoss, Nancy Leigh. *Begin at My Sanctuary: A Call to Repentance in the Church.*

———. *Freedom through Forgiveness: A practical guide to becoming a forgiven, forgiving child of God.*

———. *Is This Revival? An Appeal for Discernment.*

———. *Preparing for Revival: A Personal Spiritual Inventory based on 2 Chronicles 7:14.*

———. *Resolutions for Godly Living: Based on the Resolutions of Jonathan Edwards.*

———. *When Do We Need Revival? Fifty Evidences of the Need for a Fresh Visitation of the Spirit in Revival.* (All booklet titles available through Revive Our Hearts and Life Action Ministries.)

Elliff, Bill. *Personal Revival Checklist: Praying through the Sermon on the Mount.* Buchanan, MI: Life Action Ministries, 1990.

———. *Lifting Life's Greatest Load: How to Gain and Maintain a Clear Conscience.* Little Rock, AR: The Summit Church, 2001. (www.thesummitchurch.org)

Elliff, Bill with Tim Grissom. *Forgiveness: Healing the Harbored Hurts of Your Heart.* Little Rock, Ark.: The Summit Church, 1998. (www.thesummitchurch.org)

Elliff, Jim. *The Unrepenting Repenter* (pamphlet). Kansas City, MO: Christian Communicators Worldwide, 1994 (online: http://ccwonline.org/repent.html).

———. *Five Resolves for Personal Revival* (pamphlet). Kansas City, MO: Christian Communicators Worldwide. 1994. (online: http://ccwoline.org/5res.html).

Fehsenfeld, Del, Jr. *Fire from Heaven: Do You Want the Fire? Revive Me Series.* (Available from Life Action Ministries)

Life Action Ministries. *How to Pray for Revival.*

Paulus, Byron. *Prepare Ye the Way. Revive Me Series.* (available through Life Action Ministries)

Schlafer, Dale. *Revival 101: Understanding How Christ Ignites His Church.* Colorado Springs: Pray! Books, 2003.

Tyre, Jacquie. *Ready for Revival: A 40-Day Heart Journey Toward the Fullness of Christ.* Colorado Springs: Pray! Books, 2002.

Periodicals

Heartcry: A Journal on Revival and Spiritual Awakening. Buchanan, MI: Life Action Ministries. (www.LifeAction.org.)

Pray! Colorado Springs, Co.: NavPress. (www.praymag.com)

Reformation and Revival Journal. Carol Stream, IL: Reformation and Revival Ministries. (www.reformationrevival.com)

Spirit of Revival. Buchanan, MI: Life Action Ministries. (www.LifeAction.org.)

Audiovisual Resources

A Revival Account, Asbury 1970. Gainesville, Fla.: Reel to Real Ministries. (Video—available through Life Action Ministries.)

Cymbala, Jim. *My House Will Be a House of Prayer.* (Video—available through Life Action Ministries.)

DeMoss, Nancy Leigh. *Brokenness: The Heart God Revives.* (Also available on CD and DVD.)

———. *Call for the Wailing Women: A heart-searching message for our times from the prophet Jeremiah.*

———. *Forgiven, Forgiving, and Free!: Experiencing Freedom through the Power of Forgiveness.* (Also available on CD and DVD.)

———. *A Call to Holiness.*

———. *When Revival Comes: Discover the marks of genuine revival, illustrated in dramatic accounts from the past.* (All the above video/audiocassettes available through Revive Our Hearts and Life Action Ministries.)

Lutzer, Erwin. *The Great Awakenings.* (Audiocassette—available through Life Action Ministries.)

McLeod, Bill. *The Story of the Canadian Revival of 1971.* (Video—available through Life Action Ministries.)

Orr, Edwin J. *The Role of Prayer in Spiritual Awakening.* San Bernardino, CA: Inspirational Media. (Video—available from Campus Crusade for Christ. 1-800-352-8273.)

Peckham, Mary. *The Lewis Revival: A Personal Testimony.* (Video—available through Life Action Ministries.)

NOTE: *Go to www.SeekingHim.com to find valuable online revival resources as well as information about companion resources related to* Seeking Him *for your church or small group.*

About the **Authors**

Nancy Leigh DeMoss is the author of ten books including the bestselling *Lies Women Believe and the Truth That Sets Them Free, Choosing Forgiveness: Your Journey to Freedom,* and *Choosing Gratitude: Your Journey to Joy*. She is the host and teacher for *Revive Our Hearts* and *Seeking Him*, two nationally syndicated programs heard each weekday on over 1,000 radio stations. Through her teaching ministry and books (which have sold more than 1,600,000 copies) God is using her as a mentor and spiritual mother to thousands of women—and has positioned her as a leader of the True Woman movement.

Nancy's burden is to call women to freedom, fullness, and fruitfulness in Christ and to see God ignite true revival in the hearts of His people. For more information on her radio programs, conference ministry, and books, visit www.ReviveOurHearts.com.

Tim Grissom is a freelance writer living in Little Rock, Arkansas, where he also works as senior editor for *FamilyLife*. He has served on the elder team of The Summit Church, which he helped start in 1998, and remains active in the teaching ministry there. Tim and his wife, Janiece (who is now with the Lord) have four children. His ministry passion is to help people understand how deeply the Bible speaks to the issues of life, both big and small.

Since 1971, **Life Action Ministries** has been calling God's people to God's presence. Our family of outreaches is igniting movements of Christ-centered revival among God's people in innovative, life-changing ways:

- Summits and THIRST conferences for local **churches**
- *Revive Our Hearts* publishing, conferences, and daily radio for **women**
- Life Action Camp for **families**
- Retreats at *The Lodge* for ministry **leaders**
- *Collegiate Impact* for **universities**
- Cutting-edge resources, such as *Seeking Him* for small **groups**, *Revive* magazine and the *Infuse* podcast for personal renewal, and *Heartcry Journal* for **pastors**

Life Action Ministries
email: info@lifeaction.org
www.LifeAction.org
www.ReviveOurHearts.com

OTHER SeekingHim RESOURCES FOR YOU AND YOUR SMALL GROUP MINISTRY

- Church Package
- Small Group Package
- **SeekingHim** Women's DVD Series
- **SeekingHim** Devotions and Prayers 2 CD Set
- Pastor's Resource Kit
- Facilitator's Guide

To place your order visit us online at www.SeekingHim.com

Brought to you by:

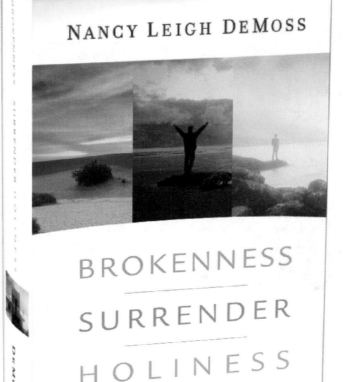